A COBOL HANDBOOK

Christopher Russell

Addison-Wesley Publishing Company
London • Reading, Massachusetts • Menlo Park, California • Amsterdam
Don Mills, Ontario • Manila • Singapore • Sydney • Tokyo

To my parents

© 1983 Addison-Wesley Publishers Limited
All rights reserved. No part of this publication may be reproduced, stored in a retrieval system, or transmitted in any form or by any means, electronic, mechanical, photocopying, recording or otherwise, without prior written permission of the publisher.

Prepared from camera-ready copy supplied by the author.

Cover design by *Margaret Hallam*
Printed in Finland by Werner Söderström Osakeyhitö. Member of Finnprint.

British Library Cataloguing in Publication Data
Russell, C.P.
   A COBOL handbook.
   1.   COBOL (Computer program language)
   I. Title
   001.64'24   QA76.73.C25

ISBN 0-201-14650-9

Library of Congress Cataloging in Publication Data
Russell, C.P. (Christopher Paul), 1953–
   A COBOL handbook

   1.   COBOL (Computer program language)   I.   Title.
QA76.73.C25R87   1983   001.64'24   83-3741
ISBN 0-201-14650-9

ABCDEF 89876543

Preface

COBOL (Common Business Orientated Language) is the most widely used commercial programming language in existence. It has been specifically designed as a tool for the computerisation of business orientated processing requirements.

This work is intended as a comprehensive handbook for COBOL. It describes all the features of COBOL and how these features are used in COBOL programs.

The book is specifically designed for ease of reference. The table of contents is listed at the front of the book and each COBOL function or element is described on its own separate page or pages. All the functions are described in the same way. That is, firstly the full format is described, then notes on usage, followed by examples of usage and lastly a blank area where the reader can insert his or her own notes. Thus, when the reader wishes to reference a COBOL verb or function he simply looks it up in the table of contents, turns to the specified page and will find all details relevant to that particular verb or function on that page.

As COBOL is a language used by nearly all commercial computers it is important that COBOL standards are maintained. If this were not the case then different computer manufacturers would adopt widely different versions of COBOL and this would destroy the language's uniformity of usage. Most manufacturers adopt ANSI standards, (American National Standards Institute), and this book is written to the latest standard, ANSI 1974.

Contents

TOPIC	PAGE
How to use this book	1
COBOL and the ANSI Standard	2
The COBOL character set	4
Notation used in format descriptions	6
COBOL program divisions	7
Columns, comments and punctuation	9
Word formation rules	11
Figurative constants	12
Conditional expressions	13
Reserved words	19
Identification Division	22
PROGRAM-ID	
AUTHOR	
INSTALLATION	
DATA-WRITTEN	
DATA-COMPILED	
SECURITY	
Environment Division	24
CONFIGURATION	26
SOURCE-COMPUTER	
OBJECT-COMPUTER	
SPECIAL-NAMES	
INPUT-OUTPUT SECTION	29
FILE-CONTROL sequential files	30
FILE-CONTROL relative files	30
FILE-CONTROL indexed files	31
I-O-CONTROL	34
Data Division	36
FILE SECTION	38
FD file description	
BLOCK CONTAINS	
RECORD CONTAINS	
LABEL RECORD	
VALUE	
DATA RECORD	
LINAGE	
CODE-SET	
REPORT	
SD Sort entry	42

TOPIC	PAGE
Data Division continued	
WORKING-STORAGE SECTION	43
LINKAGE SECTION	44
COMMUNICATION SECTION	46
CD Communication Description	
FOR INPUT	46
SYMBOLIC QUEUE	
MESSAGE DATE	
MESSAGE TIME	
SYMBOLIC SOURCE	
TEXT LENGTH	
END KEY	
STATUS KEY	
MESSAGE COUNT	
FOR OUTPUT	46
DESTINATION COUNT	
TEXT LENGTH	
STATUS KEY	
ERROR KEY	
SYMBOLIC DESTINATION	
FOR I-O	47
MESSAGE DATE	
MESSAGE TIME	
SYMBOLIC TERMINAL	
TEXT LENGTH	
END KEY	
STATUS KEY	
REPORT SECTION	54
RD Report Description	
CODE	
CONTROLS ARE	
PAGE LIMIT	
FIRST DETAIL	
LAST DETAIL	
FOOTING	

TOPIC	PAGE

Data Division continued

    Data Description Entries   58
        Level Number   66
        Data-name/FILLER   67
        REDEFINES   68
        BLANK WHEN ZERO   70
        JUSTIFIED   71
        OCCURS   72
        PICTURE   75
        SIGN   85
        SYNCHRONISED   86
        USAGE   88
        VALUE   90
        Level 66 RENAMES   92
        Level 88 condition names   93

    Report Group Description Entries   61
        LINE NUMBER
        NEXT GROUP
        TYPE
        BLANK WHEN ZERO
        COLUMN NUMBER
        GROUP
        JUSTIFIED
        PICTURE
        SOURCE
        VALUE
        SUM
        USAGE

TOPIC	PAGE
Procedure Division	95
Procedure Division WITH DECLARATIVES	98
Procedure Division Entries	
ACCEPT	100
ADD	101
ALTER	103
CALL	104
CANCEL	106
CLOSE	107
COMPUTE	108
COPY	110
CORRESPONDING option	112
DELETE	114
DISPLAY	115
DIVIDE	116
ENTER	118
EXIT	119
GENERATE, INITIATE, SUPPRESS, TERMINATE	120
GO TO (DEPENDING ON)	122
IF	123
INSPECT	125
MERGE	128
MOVE	130
MULTIPLY	134
OPEN	136
PERFORM	139
READ	142
RECEIVE, SEND, ACCEPT MESSAGE COUNT	145
RELEASE	147
RETURN	148
REWRITE	150
SEARCH	152
SET	155
SORT	156
START	158
STOP	159
STRING	160
SUBTRACT	162
UNSTRING	164
WRITE	166
APPENDIX 1 - GLOSSARY	168

HOW TO USE THIS BOOK

This book has been designed to provide a COBOL programmer with an easy to use, comprehensive handbook. It allows the user of this book to quickly reference any required COBOL function, and examine the use of that function within the program.

Each of the descriptions of COBOL functions has basically been split into four elements:-

                FORMAT
                COMMENTS
                EXAMPLES
                NOTES

The **FORMAT** defines the syntactical structure of a particular verb or function as defined by the ANSI 1974 Standard on COBOL.

The **COMMENTS** area explains the use of the particular verb or function within the program. This area also describes the implications of usage and references any other essentially related topics.

The **EXAMPLES** illustrate the real usage of the function within a program.

Although the ANSI 1974 is the standard for the COBOL language not all manufacturers use the exact standard. Some manufacturers, especially of the smaller machines, have limited ANSI capabilities, whilst others have extensions of the ANSI capabilities. For this reason a NOTES section has been included for most topics, and in this area the user may insert notes relevant to his own installation's use of COBOL.

The contents of this book are listed in the order in which they would logically appear within a program. However, the verbs within the Procedure Division, which may generally appear in any order, are described alphabetically.

The contents pages are at the front of the book and for each topic there is only one page reference. This represents the main reference, and any related topics or references are explained in the COMMENTS section.

COBOL and the ANSI Standard

COBOL is an acronym for **CO**mmon **B**usiness **O**rientated Language. It is a product of the 1960 Conference for Data Systems Languages (CODASYL).

The COBOL computer programming language is a high level procedural language used for business type applications. It's elements are based on the English language and provide a relatively machine independent method of expressing a business oriented problem to the computer.

This text is based on the American National Standards Institute (ANSI) version of COBOL, published in 1974. The 1974 standard is the latest available at this time, and represents the most widely adopted standard for COBOL.

The following extract is from the U. S. Government Printing Office Form Number 1965-0795689:

"Any organisation interested in reproducing the COBOL report and specifications in whole or part, using ideas taken from this report as the basis for an instruction manual or for any other purpose is free to do so. However, all such organisations are requested to reproduce this section as part of the introduction to the document. Those using a short passage, as in a book review, are requested to mention 'COBOL' in acknowledgment of the source, but need not quote this entire section.

"COBOL is an industry language and is not the property of any company or group of companies, or of any organisation or group of organisations.

"No warranty, expressed or implied, is made by any contributor or by the COBOL Committee as to the accuracy and functioning of the programming system and language. Moreover, no responsibility is assumed by any contributor, or by the committee, in connection therewith.

"Procedures have been established for the maintenance of COBOL. Enquiries concerning the procedures for proposing changes should be directed to the Executive Committee of the Conference on Data Systems Languages.

COBOL and the ANSI standard

"The authors and copyright holders of the copyrighted material used herein.

> FLOW-MATIC (Trademark of Sperry Rand Corporation), Programming for the UNIVAC (R) I and II, Data Automation Systems copyrighted 1958, 1959 by Sperry Rand Corporation; IBM Commercial Translator, Form No. F28-8013, copyrighted 1959 by IBM; FACT, DSI 27A5260-2760, copyrighted 1960 by Minneapolis-Honeywell.

have specifically authorised the use of this material in whole or in part, in the COBOL specifications. Such authorisation extends to the reproduction and use of COBOL specifications in programming manuals or similar publications."

COBOL character set

The ANS (American National Standard) COBOL character set consists of 51 characters, and the space character. Only these characters may be used in the actual COBOL language elements, although in the case of non-numeric literals and comments the character set can be expanded to include the computer's entire character set.

COBOL character	Meaning	Use
0-9	numbers	numeric character
A-Z	alphabet	alphabetic character
	space; blank	punctuation character
+	plus symbol	arithmetic operator; sign; editing character
-	minus symbol; hyphen	arithmetic operator; sign; editing character
*	asterisk	arithmetic operator; editing character
/	stroke; slash	arithmetic operator; editing character; line control character
=	equal sign	relational character; punctuation character
$	dollar sign	editing character
,	comma	punctuation character; editing character
;	semicolon	punctuation character
"	quotation mark	punctuation character
'	apostrophe	punctuation character
(	left parenthesis	punctuation character
)	rt parenthesis	punctuation character
<	less than	relational character
>	greater than	relational character

COBOL character set cont.

COBOL character	Meaning	Use
.	period	punctuation character; editing character

Notation used in Format Descriptions

The basic formats in this COBOL handbook are presented using a uniform system of notation. The example below of the ADD verb illustrates the notation used:

ADD {identifier-1} [indentifier-2] ...
    {literal-1   } [literal-2   ]

        TO identifier-m [rounded]...

        [on SIZE ERROR imperative statement]

COMMENTS.

The reserved words, in COBOL, are typed in capital letters. Those reserved words which in the format descriptions are underlined, are key words and must be included in the statements. Keywords which are not underlined are optional, and are provided for clarity purposes.

Words printed in lower-case letters represent information supplied by the programmer.

Curly brackets (braces) are used to enclose a compulsory item or stack of items. Square brackets are used to indicate an optional item or stack of items.

When items are stacked, only one of the items within the stack may be used.

The ellipsis (...) indicates that the preceding bracketed item can be repeated as many times as is required. Ellipsis following square brackets indicate 0 or more repetitions, and ellipsis following curly brackets indicates 1 or more repetitions.

Any arithmetic and logical operator characters (+,-,>,<,=) when appearing in the formats are required, even though they are not underlined.

All punctuation characters when shown in the formats are required by the syntax of the format. Additional punctuation characters may be inserted according to the rules for punctuation specified on Page 9.

COBOL Program Divisions

FORMAT.

    IDENTIFICATION DIVISION.

    entries

    ENVIRONMENT DIVISION.

    entries

    DATA DIVISION.

    entries

    PROCEDURE DIVISION.

    entries

COMMENTS.

Each COBOL program is divided into four basic divisions, as above. These divisions all serve a seperate purpose, and must all be present in a program.

The **IDENTIFICATION DIVISION** contains identifying information about the program. (See Page 22).

The **ENVIRONMENT DIVISION** describes the computer on which the source program is compiled, the computer on which the object program is executed, and details pertaining to the files used by the program. (See Page 24).

The **DATA DIVISION** describes all the files and areas of data which are to be used by the program. (See Page 36).

The **PROCEDURE DIVISION** contains the executable statements in the program which define the program's logic flow, and carry out all the program's operations during execution. (See Page 95).

The four divisions must appear in the above order.

COBOL Program Divisions cont.

EXAMPLE.

```
    IDENTIFICATION DIVISION.
    PROGRAM-ID. EXAMPLE.
    AUTHOR J. RILEY.

    ENVIRONMENT DIVISION.
    CONFIGURATION DIVISION.
    SOURCE-COMPUTER IBL-1990.
    OBJECT-COMPUTER IBL-1990.

    DATA DIVISION.
    WORKING-STORAGE SECTION.
    01 LINE-OUT.
        03 FILLER           PIC X(11) VALUE "MY NAME IS ".
        03 NME-OUT          PIC X(7).

    PROCEDURE DIVISION.
    START-PROG.
        MOVE "J RILEY" TO NME-OUT.
        DISPLAY LINE-OUT.
        STOP RUN.
```

NOTES.

Columns, Comments and punctuation

COLUMNS.

One line of a COBOL program contains 80 character positions. Columns 1 to 6 may be used for numerical identification of each line of coding, and columns 73 to 80 are ignored by the compiler, but as they are printed out on the program listing, may be used for identification purposes.

Lines of coding are written between column 8 and column 72. Column 8 is normally referred to as Margin A, and column 12 as Margin B. Division, section and paragraph names may be written at Margin A, and sentences at, or to the right of, Margin B. Margin A is also used in the Data Division for file and record descriptions (see Page 36).

Column 7 is used for the continuation of words from one line to the next. This is achieved by inserting a dash ("-") in column 7.

COMMENTS.

A COBOL line will be treated as a comment by the compiler if an asterisk ("*") is placed in column 7. Comments are not acted upon by the compiler and are used to insert explanatory notes into a program.

PUNCTUATION.

The COBOL punctuation characters are shown below:

PUNCTUATION CHARACTER	MEANING
	space
.	period
(	left parenthesis
)	right parenthesis
;	semicolon
,	comma
=	equal sign
"	quotation mark

Columns, Comments and Punctuation cont.

Punctuation cont.

The rules below apply to punctuation within COBOL:

- A period, semicolon or comma must not be preceded by a space, but must be followed by one.

- A space must appear between two successive words. Two or more successive spaces are treated as a single space except within non numeric literals.

- An arithmetic operator must be preceded and followed by a space.

- A comma or a semicolon may be used to seperate a series of clauses.

- A comma may be used as a seperator between the successive operands of a statement.

NOTES.

Word formation rules

A COBOL word can be a user-defined word or a reserved word. The maximum length of a COBOL word is 30 characters.

A user-defined word is one supplied by the programmer. The allowable characters are 0 to 9, A to Z and - (hyphen). The hyphen may not appear as the first or last character of a word.

The table below gives the formation rules for various types of user-defined words.

User-defined word type	formation rules
data-name file-name	Must contain at least 1 alphabetic character.
index-name mnemonic-name report-name routine-name condition-name alphabet-name	Must be unique within that type unless it can be made unique by qualification
library-name program-name text-name	Must contain at least 1 alphabetic character The first eight characters must be unique
paragraph-name section-name	May be entirely numeric Must be unique unless qualified
level numbers 01-49,66,77,88	Must be a 1 or 2 digit integer, need not be unique

Reserved words are described on page 19.

NOTES.

Figurative constants

Figurative constants are COBOL reserved words which may be used to replace certain numeric and nonnumeric literals. Below is a table of figurative constants and their equivalent literals.

Figurative constant	Literal equivalent
ZERO, ZEROES, ZEROS	The character 0 (numeric or nonnumeric)
SPACE, SPACES	Represents one or more nonnumeric space characters
HIGH-VALUE, HIGH-VALUES	Represents one or more occurrences of the character with the highest value in the collating sequence used
LOW-VALUE, LOW-VALUES	Represents one or more occurrences of the character with the lowest value in the collating sequence used
QUOTE, QUOTES	Represents one or more occurrences of the quotation mark character. Cannot be used to bound a nonnumeric literal
ALL literal	Represent one or more occurrences of the string of characters composing the literal and must be nonnumeric

A figurative constant may be used anywhere a nonnumeric literal appears in a program. Only ZERO may be used for a numeric literal.

The number of characters represented by a figurative constant when it appears in a MOVE or a comparison is equal to the length of the receiving or comparison field.

In DISPLAY, INSPECT, STRING, STOP and UNSTRING, the figurative constant has length 1, and ALL may not be used.

Conditional expressions

COMMENTS.

A conditional expression is one which may be evaluated by IF, PERFORM and SEARCH statements in a COBOL program, and may accordingly change the path of control in the program. A conditional expression may be specified as a simple or a complex condition.

Conditions may be enclosed within a parenthesis for clarity and order of evaluation purposes.

Simple Conditions

There are five simple conditions as defined below:

1. Class Conditions - A class condition determines whether a data item is alphabetic or numeric.

    Format.

          identifier IS [NOT] {NUMERIC   }
                               {ALPHABETIC}

    Items described in their PICTURE as alphabetic may not be tested to see if they are numeric or not, and items, described as numeric in their PICTURE, may not be tested as alphabetic or not.

    Valid alphabetic characters are A through Z and space. Valid numeric fields may contain any combination of the digits 0 through 9 and the operational sign, if described in the PICTURE. Numeric tests may also be carried out on edited numeric fields.

    Alphanumeric fields may be tested as numeric or alphabetic.

2. Condition-name Conditions - A condition-name condition is one in which a condition-name is defined as true or false depending on the value of the data-item it is associated with. This is performed using the level 88 condition-name feature of COBOL and is fully described on page 93.

Conditional expressions cont.

3. <u>Relation Condition</u> - A relation condition is one which causes the comparison of two operands. The operands may be either literals, identifiers or arithmetic expressions.

    Format.

    $$\text{operand-1 IS [\underline{NOT}]} \begin{Bmatrix} \underline{\text{GREATER}} \text{ THAN} \\ > \\ \underline{\text{LESS}} \text{ THAN} \\ < \\ \underline{\text{EQUAL}} \text{ TO} \\ = \end{Bmatrix} \text{operand-2}$$

    When numeric operands are compared the comparison is made in terms of algebraic value, and not the number of digits in the PICTURE of each operand. Unsigned numeric operands are considered to be positive.

    When nonnumeric operands are compared the comparison is made in terms of the collating sequence used.

    When a nonnumeric operand is compared with a numeric item, then the numeric item is considered as alphanumeric, and of the same size as the nonnumeric operand.

    Except when both operands are numeric, operand-1 and operand-2 must have the same usage. Numeric operands may have different usages. (For example, a numeric item with a DISPLAY usage may be compared with an item whose usage is COMPUTATIONAL).

4. <u>Sign Condition</u> - A sign condition determines whether a numeric operand has an algebraic value greater than, less than, or equal to zero.

Conditional expressions cont.

Format.

$$\text{operand IS } \underline{\text{NOT}} \begin{Bmatrix} \underline{\text{POSITIVE}} \\ \underline{\text{NEGATIVE}} \\ \underline{\text{ZERO}} \end{Bmatrix}$$

The operand being tested must be defined as numeric, or an arithmetic expression which evaluates to a numeric identifier.

An unsigned operand may only be POSITIVE or ZERO.

5. Switch-status condition   -   The switch-status condition is used to evaluate the on/off status of a switch as defined in the SPECIAL-NAMES paragraph. (See Page 26).

   Format.

   condition-name

   The condition-name is dealt with in the Procedure Division in the same way as level 88 condition-names.

Complex Conditions

A complex condition can be a negated simple condition or a combined condition, which can also be negated.

1. Negated Simple Conditions - A simple condition is negated by use of the logical operator NOT.

   Format.

   <u>NOT</u> simple condition

   The simple condition may not be negated if the condition itself contains the unparenthesised use of the logical operator NOT. The negated simple condition always gives the opposite to the simple condition. For example:

   NOT FIELD-1 IS EQUAL TO FIELD-2

   is true if the two fields are unequal.

Conditional expressions cont.

2. <u>Combined Conditions</u> - Combined conditions are two or more conditions connected by the logical operators AND, OR.

   Format.

   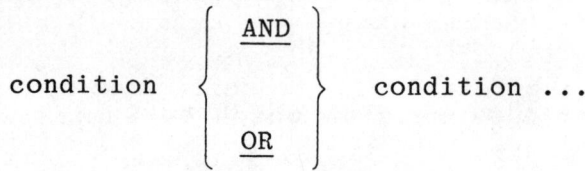

   Any of the following conditions may be combined:
   - simple conditions
   - negated simple conditions
   - combined conditions
   - a negated combined condition (combined condition in parenthesis preceded by the logical operator NOT).

   The order of truth evaluation for combined conditions is as follows:

   1. Conditions within parenthesis
   2. Arithmetic expressions
   3. Simple conditions in this order - relation
                                       - class
                                       - condition name
                                       - switch status
                                       - sign
   4. Negated simple conditions in the order given in 3.
   5. Combined conditions in this order - AND
                                        - OR
   6. Negated combined conditions in the order given in 5.
   7. Consecutive operands of the same evaluation order are evaluated left to right.

   See examples.

Conditional expressions cont.

EXAMPLES.

<u>Simple conditions</u>

    Class.

    IF A IS ALPHABETIC GO TO NEXT-TEST.
    IF B NOT NUMERIC GO TO ERROR-IN-B.

    Condition-name.

    IF MONTH-OK PERFORM DATE-PRINT.

    Relation.

    PERFORM ROUTINES-1 UNTIL FIELD-1 IS GREATER THAN 50.
    IF LINE-NO IS NOT GREATER THAN 50 PERFORM LINE-PARA.

    Sign.

    IF TEMP IS NEGATIVE DISPLAY "IT'S FREEZING".

    Switch-status.

    IF STATUS-OKAY NEXT SENTENCE.

<u>Complex-Conditions.</u>

    Negated simple.

    IF NOT FIELD-1 IS NUMERIC GO TO ERROR-ROUTINE.

    IF NOT A > B ADD A TO B.

    Combined conditions.

    IF SWITCH-1 = "OFF" AND SWITCH-2 = "OFF"
                       DISPLAY "SWITCH FAULT".

    IF A = 1 AND (B = 1 OR C = 1) GO TO END-ROUTINE.

Conditional expressions cont.

EXAMPLES cont.

Combined conditions cont.

IF NOT A + B > C OR (SW-1 AND SW-2 = 1) GO TO
                                              PARA-A.

The above expression is evaluated in the following order:
1. SW-1 and SW-2 are checked for equality to 1.
2. The expression A+B is evaluated.
3. The result of A+B is checked if greater than C and if it is not it's condition is said to be true.
4. If either 1 or 3 above are evaluated as true control is passed to PARA-A.

NOTES.

RESERVED WORDS

The following is the full set of reserved words according to ANSI 74 standards. A reserved word has a particular meaning in COBOL and may not be used for a programmer defined name. For example ADD is the addition verb in COBOL and therefore may not be used as a data-name or procedure-name as it would confuse the compiler.

ACCEPT	COMPUTATIONAL	DYNAMIC
ACCESS	COMPUTE	EGI
ADD	CONFIGURATION	ELSE
ADVANCING	CONTAINS	EMI
AFTER	CONTROL	ENABLE
ALL	CONTROLS	END
ALPHABETIC	COPY	END-OF-PAGE
ALSO	CORR	ENTER
ALTER	CORRESPONDING	ENVIRONMENT
ALTERNATIVE	COUNT	EOP
AND	CURRENCY	EQUAL
ARE	DATA	ERROR
AREA	DATE	ESI
AREAS	DATE-COMPILED	EVERY
ASCENDING	DATE-WRITTEN	EXCEPTION
ASSIGN	DAY	EXIT
AT	DE	EXTEND
AUTHOR	DEBUG-CONTENTS	FD
BEFORE	DEBUG-ITEM	FILE
BLANK	DEBUG-LINE	FILE-CONTROL
BLOCK	DEBUG-NAME	FILLER
BOTTOM	DEBUG-SUB-1	FINAL
BY	DEBUG-SUB-2	FIRST
CALL	DEBUG-SUB-3	FOOTING
CANCEL	DEBUGGING	FOR
CD	DECIMAL POINT	FROM
CF	DECLARATIVES	GENERATE
CH	DELETE	GIVING
CHARACTER	DELIMITED	GO
CHARACTERS	DELIMITER	GREATER
CLOCK-UNITS	DEPENDING	GROUP
CLOSE	DESCENDING	HEADING
COBOL	DESTINATION	HIGH-VALUE
CODE	DETAIL	HIGH-VALUES
CODE-SET	DISABLE	I-O
COLLATING	DISPLAY	I-O-CONTROL
COLUMN	DIVIDE	IDENTIFICATION
COMMA	DIVISION	IF
COMMUNICATION	DOWN	IN
COMP	DUPLICATES	INDEX

RESERVED WORDS cont.

INDEXED	ON	REWIND
INDICATE	OPEN	REWRITE
INITIAL	OPTIONAL	RF
INITIATE	OR	RH
INPUT	ORGANISATION	RIGHT
INPUT-OUTPUT	OUTPUT	ROUNDED
INSPECT	OVERFLOW	RUN
INSTALLATION	PAGE	SAME
INTO	PAGE-COUNTER	SD
INVALID	PERFORM	SEARCH
IS	PF	SECTION
JUST	PH	SECURITY
JUSTIFIED	PIC	SEGMENT-LIMIT
KEY	PICTURE	SELECT
LABEL	PLUS	SEND
LEADING	POINTER	SENTENCE
LEFT	POSITION	SEPERATE
LENGTH	POSITIVE	SEQUENCE
LESS	PRINTING	SEQUENTIAL
LIMIT	PROCEDURE	SET
LIMITS	PROCEDURES	SIGN
LINAGE	PROCEED	SIZE
LINAGE-COUNTER	PROGRAM	SORT
LINE	PROGRAM-ID	SORT-MERGE
LINE-COUNTER	QUEUE	SOURCE
LINES	QUOTE	SOURCE-COMPUTER
LINKAGE	QUOTES	SPACE
LOCK	RANDOM	SPACES
LOW-VALUE	RD	SPECIAL-NAMES
LOW-VALUES	READ	STANDARD
MEMORY	RECIEVE	STANDARD-1
MERGE	RECORD	START
MESSAGE	RECORDS	STATUS
MODE	REDEFINES	STOP
MODULES	REEL	STRING
MOVE	REFERENCES	SUB-QUEUE-1
MULTIPLE	RELATIVE	SUB-QUEUE-2
MULTIPLY	RELEASE	SUB-QUEUE-3
NATIVE	REMAINDER	SUBTRACT
NEGATIVE	REMOVAL	SUM
NEXT	RENAMES	SUPPRESS
NO	REPLACING	SYMBOLIC
NOT	REPORT	SYNC
NUMBER	REPORTING	SYNCHRONISED
NUMERIC	REPORTS	TABLE
OBJECT-COMPUTER	RERUN	TALLYING
OCCURS	RESERVE	TAPE
OF	RESET	TERMINAL
OFF	RETURN	TERMINATE
OMITTED	REVERSED	TEXT

RESERVED WORDS cont.

THAN	UNSTRING	WHEN
THROUGH	UNTIL	WITH
THRU	UP	WORDS
TIME	UPON	WORKING-STORAGE
TIMES	USAGE	WRITE
TO	USE	ZERO
TOP	USING	ZEROES
TRAILING	VALUE	ZEROS
TYPE	VALUES	
UNIT	VARYING	

IDENTIFICATION DIVISION

FORMAT.

    <u>IDENTIFICATION DIVISION</u>.

    <u>PROGRAM-ID</u>. Program-name.

    [<u>AUTHOR</u>. comment-entry]

    [<u>INSTALLATION</u>. [comment-entry]...]

    [<u>DATE-WRITTEN</u>. [comment-entry]...]

    [<u>DATE-COMPILED</u>. [comment-entry]...]

    [<u>SECURITY</u>. [comment-entry]...]

COMMENTS.

The IDENTIFICATION DIVISION must appear as the first division in the program. It identifies the program, the author, and gives other program details. Only the PROGRAM-ID is compulsory, and the program name must conform to the rules for the implementation used.

The contents of the other paragraphs are ignored by the compiler (although they appear on the object program listing) except the DATE-COMPILED paragraph, which has its comment-entry replaced by the current date at compilation time.

IDENTIFICATION DIVISION cont.

EXAMPLE.

    .
```
    IDENTIFICATION DIVISION.
    PROGRAM-ID. PROG1.
    AUTHOR. C RUSSELL.
    INSTALLATION. NOTTINGHAM.
    DATE WRITTEN. 10 DEC 1983.
    DATE COMPILED. TO BE INSERTED.
    SECURITY. THIS PROGRAM IS TO BE COPIED TWICE EACH
              UPDATE  AND  THE  COPIES  KEPT  IN  THE
              SECURITY VAULTS.
    ENVIRONMENT DIVISION.
```
    .
    .
    .

NOTES.

ENVIRONMENT DIVISION

FORMAT.

    <u>ENVIRONMENT DIVISION</u>.

    <u>CONFIGURATION SECTION</u>.

    <u>SOURCE-COMPUTER</u>. computer-name.

    <u>OBJECT-COMPUTER</u>. computer-name.

    [<u>SPECIAL-NAMES</u>. entry.]

    [<u>INPUT-OUTPUT SECTION</u>.

    <u>FILE-CONTROL</u>. file-control entry.

     [file-control entry]...

    [<u>I-O-CONTROL</u>. input-output-control entry]]

COMMENTS.

The Environment Division provides details on the type of computer being used, and the relationship between the logical concept of the files as defined in the program, and the physical aspects of the files, as stored externally.

The above format is general and is further broken down on subsequent pages.

The Environment Division may contain 2 sections. The Configuration Section describes on which computer the source and object programs are to be held. It can also, in the Special-Names paragraph, relate user defined mnemonic-names to specific devices or device actions.

The Input-Output Section is used to define the files and external media required by the program, and to provide information on the handling of data during the program's execution.

ENVIRONMENT DIVISION cont.

EXAMPLE.

```
    .
    .
ENVIRONMENT DIVISION.
CONFIGURATION SECTION.
SOURCE-COMPUTER. IBL-1960.
OBJECT-COMPUTER. IBL-1960.
SPECIAL-NAMES.   CURRENCY SIGN IS "£".
INPUT-OUTPUT SECTION.
FILE-CONTROL.
    SELECT PRINT FILE ASSIGN TO PRINTER.
    SELECT IN-FILE ASSIGN TO DISK
         ORGANISATION IS SEQUENTIAL.
```

NOTES.

ENVIRONMENT DIVISION   **CONFIGURATION SECTION**

FORMAT.

<u>CONFIGURATION SECTION</u>.

<u>SOURCE-COMPUTER</u>. computer-name [WITH <u>DEBUGGING MODE</u>].

<u>OBJECT-COMPUTER</u>. computer-name

      [<u>MEMORY</u> SIZE integer $\begin{Bmatrix} \underline{WORDS} \\ \underline{CHARACTERS} \\ \underline{MODULES} \end{Bmatrix}$]

      [PROGRAM COLLATING <u>SEQUENCE</u> IS alphabet-name]

      [<u>SEGMENT-LIMIT</u> IS segment-number].

[<u>SPECIAL-NAMES</u>.

   [implementor-name-1 IS mnemonic-name]...

   [implementor-name-2 [IS mnemonic-name]

$\begin{Bmatrix} \begin{matrix} \underline{ON}\ STATUS\ \underline{IS}\ condition\text{-}name\text{-}1 \\ [\underline{OFF}\ STAT\overline{US}\ \underline{IS}\ condition\text{-}name\text{-}2] \end{matrix} \\ \begin{matrix} \underline{OFF}\ STATUS\ \underline{IS}\ condition\text{-}name\text{-}2 \\ [\underline{ON}\ STATUS\ \overline{IS}\ condition\text{-}name\text{-}1] \end{matrix} \end{Bmatrix}$]...

[alphabet-name IS $\begin{Bmatrix} \underline{STANDARD\text{-}1} \\ \underline{NATIVE} \\ implementor\text{-}name\text{-}3 \\ literal\text{-}1 \begin{bmatrix} \underline{THRU}\ lit\text{-}2 \\ \underline{ALSO}\ lit\text{-}3 \\ \quad [\underline{ALSO}\ lit\text{-}4]... \end{bmatrix}... \end{Bmatrix}$ ...]

[<u>CURRENCY</u> SIGN <u>IS</u> literal-5]

[<u>DECIMAL-POINT</u> <u>IS</u> <u>COMMA</u>].]

ENVIRONMENT DIVISION   CONFIGURATION SECTION cont.

COMMENTS.

The CONFIGURATION SECTION describes the computers on which the program is to be compiled and run, and also relates implementor-names to programmer-defined mnemonic-names.

The SOURCE-COMPUTER paragraph identifies the computer on which the object program is to be compiled. If the DEBUGGING MODE option is used then the program debug facilities will be available for use.

The OBJECT-COMPUTER paragraph identifies the computer on which the program is to be executed. The MEMORY SIZE option is used to give the amount of main memory needed for the program's execution.

The SEGMENT-LIMIT clause is used in conjunction with the Sections in the Procedure Division. Sections may be given priority of use numbers; the lower a number, the more often it is used. The SEGMENT-LIMIT indicates a priority number below which all Sections (or segments) are permanently resident in the main-storage for the duration of the run.

The SPECIAL-NAMES paragraph relates computer-defined implementor-names to programmer-defined mnemonic names. It can also specify a collating sequence to be associated with an alphabet-name, and may also specify an alternative currency sign and comma as an alternative decimal point in PICTURE clauses.

Implementor-name-1 refers to a system device or a standard system action which may be given a programmer-defined mnemonic-name. The mnemonic-name may then be used with the ACCEPT, DISPLAY, SEND and WRITE verbs.

Implementor-name-2 refers to a one-byte program switch, as defined for the particular computer in use. The associated condition-name is used in the Procedure Division to check the Status of the switch and the associated mnemonic-name, if specified, is used for qualification purposes. (See Page 13).

ENVIRONMENT DIVISION　　　　　**CONFIGURATION SECTION cont.**

COMMENTS cont.

The alphabet-name clause is used to relate an alphabet-name to a specific character-code-set or collating-sequence. When used for the collating-sequence the alphabet-name must correspond to that given in the OBJECT-COMPUTER paragraph.
When STANDARD-1 is used the code set or collating sequence used is the ASCII character set, and when NATIVE is used the EBCDIC character set is used.
When implementor-name-3 is used the collating sequence is specified by a standard system action defined on the particular computer in use.
When the literal option is used the collating sequence is defined by the programmer.
When the CURRENCY SIGN option is used an alternative currency sign may be used.
When the DECIMAL-POINT option is used the comma and decimal-points are interchanged in PICTURE strings.

EXAMPLES.

```
    CONFIGURATION SECTION.
    SOURCE-COMPUTER. IBL-1990 WITH DEBUGGING MODE.
    OBJECT-COMPUTER. IBL-1990 MEMORY SIZE 15000
                                            CHARACTERS
                       PROGRAMMING COLLATING SEQUENCE IS
                                            CODE-NM
                       SEGMENT LIMIT IS 0.
    SPECIAL NAMES.
       PAGE IS NEW-FORM
       UPSI-1 ON STATUS IS SWITCH-ON
           OFF STATUS IS SWITCH-OFF
       CODE-NM IS NATIVE
       CURRENCY SIGN IS "£"
       DECIMAL POINT IS COMMA.
```

NOTES

ENVIRONMENT DIVISION   **INPUT-OUTPUT SECTION**

FORMAT.

   [<u>INPUT-OUTPUT SECTION</u>.

   <u>FILE-CONTROL</u>. file-control entry

          [file-control entry]...

   [<u>I-O-CONTROL</u>. input-output-control entry]]

COMMENTS.

The INPUT-OUTPUT SECTION is required by all COBOL programs unless they do not require an input or an output file.

The FILE-CONTROL paragraph associates each file with an external peripheral device and defines its organisation, access mode and other information.

The I-O-CONTROL paragraph is optional within this section, and specifies shared file areas, location of certain files on multi-file reel, and specifies when checkpoints are taken for restart purposes.

Both these paragraphs are described on the following pages.

EXAMPLE.

```
   INPUT-OUTPUT SECTION.
   FILE-CONTROL.
       SELECT PRINT-FILE ASSIGN TO PRINTER.
       SELECT IN-FILE-A ASSIGN TO DISK.
       SELECT IN-FILE-B ASSIGN TO DISK.
   I-O-CONTROL.
       SAME AREA FOR IN-FILE-A IN-FILE-B.
```

NOTES.

ENVIRONMENT DIV.   INPUT-OUTPUT SECTION   FILE-CONTROL

FORMAT.

<u>FILE-CONTROL</u>.

Format-1 : Sequential Organisation

<u>SELECT</u> [<u>OPTIONAL</u>] file-name
              <u>ASSIGN</u> TO implementor-name-1
                      [implementor-name-2]...

    [<u>RESERVE</u> integer $\begin{bmatrix} AREA \\ AREAS \end{bmatrix}$]

    [<u>ORGANISATION</u> IS <u>SEQUENTIAL</u>]

    [<u>ACCESS</u> MODE IS <u>SEQUENTIAL</u>]

    [FILE <u>STATUS</u> IS data-name].

Format-2 : Relative Organisation

<u>SELECT</u> file-name <u>ASSIGN</u> TO implementor-name-1
                      [implementor-name-2]...

    [<u>RESERVE</u> integer $\begin{bmatrix} AREA \\ AREAS \end{bmatrix}$]

    <u>ORGANISATION</u> IS <u>RELATIVE</u>

$$[\underline{ACCESS}\ MODE\ IS \begin{Bmatrix} \underline{SEQUENTIAL}\ [\underline{RELATIVE}\ KEY\ IS \\ \qquad\qquad\qquad\qquad\text{data-name-1}] \\ \underline{RANDOM}\ \ \ \underline{RELATIVE}\ KEY\ IS \\ \qquad\qquad\qquad\text{data-name-2} \\ \underline{DYNAMIC} \end{Bmatrix}]$$

    [FILE <u>STATUS</u> IS data-name-2].

ENVIRONMENT DIVISION   **FILE-CONTROL cont.**

FORMAT cont.

Format-3 : Indexed Organisation

<u>SELECT</u> file-name <u>ASSIGN</u> TO implementor-name-1
                                [implementor-name-2]...

    [<u>RESERVE</u> integer [AREA]]
                       [AREAS]

    <u>ORGANISATION</u> IS <u>INDEXED</u>

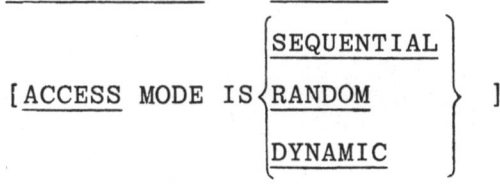

                     ⎧<u>SEQUENTIAL</u>⎫
    [<u>ACCESS</u> MODE IS ⎨<u>RANDOM</u>   ⎬]
                     ⎩<u>DYNAMIC</u>   ⎭

    <u>RECORD</u> KEY IS data-name-1

    [<u>ALTERNATE</u> <u>RECORD</u> KEY IS data-name-2
                          [WITH <u>DUPLICATES</u>]]...
    [FILE <u>STATUS</u> IS data-name-3].

COMMENTS.

The FILE-CONTROL paragraph associates each file in the program with a particular peripheral device (such as the printer) and defines the organisation, access mode and other specific points associated with the file.

Each file specified with a SELECT clause must have a corresponding FD or SD clause in the Data Division. The OPTIONAL entry may only be specified for sequential files which need not be present at execution time.

The mandatory ASSIGN clause is used to associate that particular file with a specific peripheral device, as named for the type of computer in use.

The RESERVE clause is used to state the number of buffers required for a file. The number of buffers allocated is normally carried out by the system, but the RESERVE clause may be used to possibly cut down the number of buffers used, and thus save space, although this would probably slow down execution.

ENVIRONMENT DIVISION   **FILE-CONTROL cont.**

COMMENTS cont.

The ORGANISATION clause is used to specify how the file is organised, and is mandatory, except when the organisation is SEQUENTIAL, in which case the default may be used.

The ACCESS MODE defines how the program is to access the data held in the file. Files which are organised sequentially may only be accessed sequentially. Files which are organised in a relative or indexed manner may be accessed sequentially, randomly or dynamically.

For relative files a RELATIVE KEY must be defined which gives the desired record number counting from the beginning of the file. The data-name associated with the RELATIVE KEY is an unsigned integer data-item defined in the Working-Storage Section.

For indexed files the RECORD KEY defines the data-item within the record that gives the key for its indexed location. It must be defined as a fixed length alphanumeric field. The indexed file may also have an ALTERNATE RECORD KEY clause which allows the defining of an alternative location key. The WITH DUPLICATES option allows a duplicate key entry to be made. With sequential access duplicate records are retrieved in the order they were placed in the file, and in random access only the first of a set of duplicate key records can be retrieved.

The FILE STATUS clause allows the status of a file to be checked after each input-output request is made on the file. After each input-output request the system moves a code into the data item defined by the FILE STATUS clause. This code can then be checked and will indicate file conditions such as file corrupt, file not found etc. The code itself is normally a two digit alphanumeric field and the meaning of each code will vary from machine to machine.

ENVIRONMENT DIVISION   **FILE CONTROL cont.**

EXAMPLES.

```
    .
    SELECT SEQ-FILE ASSIGN TO DISK
                    RESERVE 4 AREAS
                    ORGANISATION IS SEQUENTIAL
                    ACCESS MODE IS SEQUENTIAL
                    FILE STATUS IS STATUS-BYTES.
    SELECT REL-FILE ASSIGN TO DISK
                    ORGANISATION IS RELATIVE
                    ACCESS MODE IS RANDOM RELATIVE KEY
                       IS REC-KEY.
    SELECT IND-FILE ASSIGN TO DISK
                    ORGANISATION IS INDEXED
                    ACCESS MODE IS DYNAMIC.

 .
 SELECT TAPE-FILE ASSIGN TO TAPE READER.
 .
 SELECT PRINT-FILE ASSIGN TO PRINTER.
```

NOTES.

ENVIRONMENT DIV.   INPUT-OUTPUT SECTION   I-O-CONTROL

FORMAT.

I-O-CONTROL.

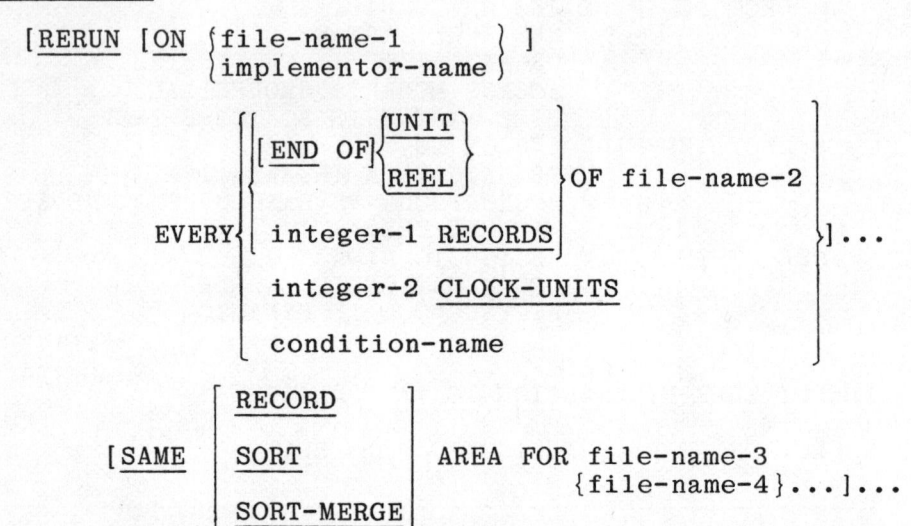

    [RERUN [ON $\begin{Bmatrix} \text{file-name-1} \\ \text{implementor-name} \end{Bmatrix}$]

$$\text{EVERY} \begin{Bmatrix} [\text{END OF}] \begin{Bmatrix} \text{UNIT} \\ \text{REEL} \end{Bmatrix} \text{OF file-name-2} \\ \text{integer-1 RECORDS} \\ \text{integer-2 CLOCK-UNITS} \\ \text{condition-name} \end{Bmatrix}] \ldots$$

    [SAME $\begin{bmatrix} \text{RECORD} \\ \text{SORT} \\ \text{SORT-MERGE} \end{bmatrix}$ AREA FOR file-name-3 {file-name-4}...]...

    [MULTIPLE FILE TAPE CONTAINS

        file-name-5 [POSITION integer-3]

        {file-name-6 [POSITION integer-4]}...]... .

COMMENTS.

The I-O-CONTROL paragraph is optional in a COBOL program. When included it specifies when checkpoints are to be taken for restart purposes, which files are to share areas, and the positioning of certain files on multi-file reels.

The RERUN clause specifies that checkpoint records are to be written to a certain peripheral. These records may be written at the end of each file or REEL, after integer RECORDS or CLOCK-UNITS, or after a specified condition becomes true. This means that restarts may be made, in the event of a failure, from the last checkpoint.

The SAME clause specifies which files may share main-storage areas during program execution. This clause

ENVIRONMENT DIVISION

COMMENTS cont.

will allow the transfer of data from one area to another with very little data manipulation as the input/output areas of the files are the same. This feature should be used for files in the program which require simple input to output action, sort action, or merge actions.

The MULTIPLE FILE clause specifies the position of a file within a multiple file reel. It may also, more simply, be used to indicate the names of files held on a multi-file reel. This option only serves as documentation unless the files have non-standard labels, or if the labels are omitted.

The POSITION integer refers to the beginning tape mark of a file. For example, as each file has tape marks at the beginning and end, then for a reel containing two non-standard header files, the beginning positions would be 1 and 3.

EXAMPLES.

```
 I-O-CONTROL.
     RERUN ON TAPE-BACKUP-FILE-A EVERY 500 RECORDS OF
                                 IN-FILE
     RERUN ON TAPE-BACKUP-FILE-B EVERY PROG-FAIL

     SAME RECORD AREA FOR IN-FILE, OUT-FILE

     MULTIPLE FILE CONTAINS FILE-A POSITION 1
                            FILE-B POSITION 3.
```

NOTES.

DATA DIVISION

FORMAT.

   DATA DIVISION.

   [FILE SECTION.

   [file-description entry
   [record-description entry]...]...]

   [WORKING-STORAGE SECTION.

   ⎡77-level-description entry⎤ ...]
   ⎣record-description entry   ⎦

   [LINKAGE SECTION.

   ⎡77-level-description entry⎤ ...]
   ⎣record-description entry   ⎦

   [COMMUNICATION SECTION.

   [communication description entry
   [record-description entry]...]...]

   [REPORT SECTION.

   [report-description entry
   [report-group description entry]...]...]

COMMENTS.

The DATA DIVISION describes all the data to be processed by the object program.

Each of the sections is optional although if included must appear in the given order.

The FILE SECTION describes all the files and associated records in the program. The WORKING-STORAGE SECTION describes any internal data used by the program during execution. The LINKAGE SECTION is used only when the program is to be called by another program. It defines the data common to both programs. The COMMUNICATION SECTION contains the communication-description entries for input and output to the system's message

DATA DIVISION cont.

COMMENTS cont.

controlling system. The REPORT section is used to describe the characteristics of any reports to be generated by the program.

The individual sections are described on the following pages.

EXAMPLES.

There are no examples for this page.

NOTES.

DATA DIVISION   FILE SECTION FD Entries

FORMAT.

FILE SECTION.

[FD file-name

    [BLOCK CONTAINS [integer-1 TO]
                           integer-2 $\begin{Bmatrix} \text{CHARACTERS} \\ \text{RECORDS} \end{Bmatrix}$]

    [RECORD CONTAINS [integer-3 TO]
                           integer-4 CHARACTERS]

    LABEL $\begin{Bmatrix} \text{RECORD IS} \\ \text{RECORDS ARE} \end{Bmatrix} \begin{Bmatrix} \text{STANDARD} \\ \text{OMITTED} \end{Bmatrix}$

    [VALUE OF implementor-name-1 IS $\begin{Bmatrix} \text{data-name-1} \\ \text{literal-1} \end{Bmatrix}$

        [implementor-name-2 IS $\begin{Bmatrix} \text{data-name-2} \\ \text{literal-2} \end{Bmatrix}$]...]

    [DATA $\begin{Bmatrix} \text{RECORD IS} \\ \text{RECORDS ARE} \end{Bmatrix}$ data-name-3 [data-name-4]...]

    [LINAGE IS $\begin{Bmatrix} \text{data-name-5} \\ \text{integer-5} \end{Bmatrix}$ LINES

        [WITH FOOTING AT $\begin{Bmatrix} \text{data-name-6} \\ \text{integer-6} \end{Bmatrix}$]

        [LINES AT TOP $\begin{Bmatrix} \text{data-name-7} \\ \text{integer-7} \end{Bmatrix}$]

        [LINES AT BOTTOM $\begin{Bmatrix} \text{data-name-8} \\ \text{integer-8} \end{Bmatrix}$]

    [CODE-SET IS alphabet-name

    [$\begin{Bmatrix} \text{REPORT IS} \\ \text{REPORTS ARE} \end{Bmatrix}$ report-name-1 [report-name-2]...].

    [record-description entry]...]...

DATA DIVISION   **FILE SECTION FD entries cont.**

COMMENTS.

Within the FILE SECTION there are two major entries, the file description entry (FD) and the sort-file description entry (SD). The FD entry is described here and the SD entry on page 42.

The FD entry provides information on the physical structure and identification of a file and gives the RECORD names associated with that file. All files to be used in a program must be specified with an FD entry.

The file-name must correspond to the programmer defined file-name specified in the SELECT entry of the INPUT-OUTPUT SECTION.

All FD entries are optional except the LABEL RECORD(S) clause, and they may appear in any order.

The BLOCK CONTAINS clause specifies the size of a physical record. The size may be specified in either characters or records, characters being the default. When this clause is omitted the compiler assumes the records are not blocked (i.e. each physical record contains only one logical record).

The RECORD CONTAINS clause is used to specify the size of a file's associated data record. This clause is always optional as the record description entry defines the size of each record.

The LABEL RECORDS clause is required by each FD entry. It specifies whether labels are present on the file. The STANDARD option must be given for disk files and the OMITTED option must be specified for files assigned to unit record devices such as the printer. Magnetic tape files may, or may not, have labels.

The VALUE clause associates a name with a particular item on the file's header label. It may, therefore, only be specified when label records have been defined as standard. It is normally used to associate a particular FD statement with the name defined on a file's header label.

The DATA RECORDS clause is used to indicate record description entries associated with a file. The record description entries themselves are defined after the FD statement.

DATA DIVISION   **FILE SECTION FD Entries cont.**

COMMENTS cont.

The LINEAGE clause can only be used with files assigned to the printer. It specifies the size of a logical page, in terms of number of lines. It also specifies the size of the TOP and BOTTOM margins, and the line number within the page body at which a footing area begins. The total page size is the sum of all the values in each phrase except for FOOTING. The page sizes are set upon execution of the OPEN statement. The FOOTING area (for totals etc.) is used by the imperative statements of the WRITE ... AT END-OF-PAGE statement. (See Page 166).

The REPORT clause specifies the names of any reports associated with the file. This clause is associated with the Report Writer capabilities of COBOL and is described in more detail under REPORT SECTION (See Page 54).

The CODE-SET clause is used to identify the character code convention used to represent DISPLAY-type data on external media. The CODE-SET clause may only be used for non-mass-storage files and the alphabet-name must be defined in the SPECIAL-NAMES paragraph.

The record-description entries follow the FD statement and are described in detail under the Data Description Entries starting on page 58.

EXAMPLES.
   •
   •
```
   FD  PRINTFILE
       RECORD CONTAINS 123 CHARACTERS
       LABEL RECORDS ARE OMITTED
       DATA RECORD IS PRINTREC
       LINAGE IS 50 LINES
               WITH FOOTING AT 40
               LINES AT TOP      5
               LINES AT BOTTOM   5.

   01  PRINTREC.
       03 FILLER               PIC X(10).
       03 EMP-NAME             PIC X(20).
```
   •
   •
   •

DATA DIVISION   **FILE SECTION FD Entries cont.**

EXAMPLES cont.

```
     .
     .
     FD  TAPEFILE
         BLOCK CONTAINS 10 RECORDS
         LABEL RECORDS STANDARD
         VALUE OF FILE-ID IS "TAPEMASTER"
         DATA RECORDS ARE INPUT-1, INPUT-2.
     01  INPUT-1.
         03  ITEM-A              PIC X(5).
     .
     .
     .
     01  INPUT-2.
         03  NUM-A               PIC 9(8).
     .
     .
     .
     FD  DISKFILE
         LABEL RECORDS ARE STANDARD.
     01  DISK-REC.
         03  IN-A                PIC 9.
     .
     .
     .
```

NOTES.

DATA DIVISION   **FILE SECTION SD Entries.**

FORMAT.

[SD file-name

   [<u>RECORD</u> CONTAINS [integer-1 <u>TO</u>] integer-2 CHARACTERS]

   [<u>DATA</u> {<u>RECORD</u> IS / <u>RECORDS</u> ARE} data-name-1 [data-name-2]...].

   {record-description entry}...]

COMMENTS.

The SD entry is associated with the sort/merge facility of COBOL. When carrying out the sort/merge operation a FD entry has to be made for each file input to, or output from the operation. There must also be a SD (sort-merge-file description) and associated record description for each sort or merge file in the program.

Further details of use are given in the MERGE and SORT verb descriptions on pages 128 and 156 respectively.

EXAMPLE.

```
    SD  SORT-FILE.
    01  SORT-REC.
        03 KEY-1              PIC X(5).
        03 REST-REC           PIC X(75).
    FD  INFILE
        LABEL RECORD STANDARD.
    01  REC-IN                PIC X(80).
    FD  OUTFILE
        LABEL RECORD STANDARD.
    01  REC-OUT               PIC X(80).

    PROCEDURE DIVISION.

        SORT SORT-FILE ON ASCENDING KEY-1 USING INFILE
                                       GIVING OUTFILE.
```

NOTES.

DATA DIVISION   WORKING STORAGE SECTION

FORMAT.

[<u>WORKING-STORAGE</u> SECTION.

[77-level-description entry] ...]
[record-description entry]

COMMENTS.

Data items which are used during the execution of a program but are not part of a file are held in the WORKING-STORAGE SECTION. The data items held in this section may use the Level numbers 01-49 and level 77. Detailed descriptions of each element of the WORKING-STORAGE SECTION may be found under Data Description Entries starting on page 58.

The initial value of items within Working Storage is unpredictable, and so items requiring an initial value should be initialised using the VALUE clause in Working Storage, or an appropriate Procedure Division Verb.

The WORKING-STORAGE SECTION is not compulsory and within it level 77 and level 01 items may be inserted in any order.

EXAMPLES.

```
    .
    WORKING-STORAGE SECTION.
    77 PAGE-COUNTER            PIC 9 VALUE ZERO.
    77 LINE-COUNTER            PIC 99 VALUE ZERO.
    01 HOLDING-FIELDS.
       03 TOTAL-A              PIC 99 VALUE 0.
       03 TOTAL-B              PIC 99 VALUE 0.
       03 TOTAL-C              PIC 99 VAULE 0.
    .
    77 AMOUNT                  PIC 99V99.
    .
```

NOTES.

DATA DIVISION   LINKAGE SECTION

FORMAT.

[LINKAGE SECTION.

[77-level-description entry] ...]
 record description entry

COMMENTS.

The LINKAGE SECTION is only included in a program when it is to be called by another program. It describes the data items which are common to both the called program and the calling program.

Storage space is not allocated to these items within the LINKAGE SECTION, it merely provides a link to the data items which reside in the calling program. Consequently, VALUE clauses may not be used in this section except for those associated with level-88 condition names.

Apart from the VALUE clause the LINKAGE SECTION may contain any data description clause.

In general, the calling program does not have a LINKAGE SECTION unless it, too, is a called program. In the calling program the common data items are defined in the File or Working-Storage Sections.

Data items common to both programs need not have the same name and data description, although they must contain the same number of characters.

In the called program's Procedure Division the common data items are identified by means of the USING option of the Procedure Division header (see Page 95), whilst in the calling program the common data items are identified by means of the USING option of the CALL verb (see Page 104).

DATA DIVISION   **LINKAGE SECTION cont.**

EXAMPLE.

Called program description
  .
  LINKAGE SECTION.
  01 NAM-LIST.
     03 INITS   PIC XX.
     03 SURNAM   PIC X(15).
  .
  .
  .
  PROCEDURE DIVISION USING NAM-LIST.
  .
  .

Called program description
  .
  WORKING-STORAGE SECTION.
  01 EMP-DETS.
  05 INIT-1   PIC A.
  05 INIT-2   PIC A.
  05 NAM-IN   PIC X(15).
  .
  .
  PROCEDURE DIVISION.
  .
  .
       CALL CALLED-PROG USING EMP-DETS.
  .

NOTES.

DATA DIVISION   COMMUNICATION SECTION

FORMAT.

  [COMMUNICATION SECTION.

Format 1.

CD   cd-name-1 FOR INPUT

              [SYMBOLIC QUEUE IS data-name-1]

              [MESSAGE DATE IS data-name-2]

              [MESSAGE TIME IS data-name-3]

              [SYMBOLIC SOURCE IS data-name-4]

              [TEXT LENGTH IS data-name-5]

              [END KEY IS data-name-6]

              [STATUS KEY IS data-name-7]

              [MESSAGE COUNT IS data-name-8].

Format 2.

CD   cd-name-1 FOR OUTPUT

              [DESTINATION COUNT IS data-name-1]

              [TEXT LENGTH IS data-name-2]

              [STATUS KEY IS data-name-3]

              [ERROR KEY IS data-name-4]

              [SYMBOLIC DESTINATION IS data-name-5].

DATA DIVISION **COMMUNICATION SECTION cont.**

FORMAT cont.

Format 3.

   CD   cd-name-1 FOR I-O

                  [MESSAGE DATA IS data name-1]

                  [MESSAGE TIME IS data-name-2]

                  [SYMBOLIC TERMINAL IS data-name-3]

                  [TEXT LENGTH IS data-name-4]

                  [END KEY IS data-name-5]

                  [STATUS KEY IS data-name-6].

COMMENTS.

The communication feature of COBOL provides the ability to access, process and create messages, and communicate with the system via an MCS (message control system).

The feature described here is the ANSI level 1 Communication feature and within the Procedure Division allows the RECEIVE, SENT and ACCEPT MESSAGE COUNT statements to be used.

Format 1.

This CD entry specifies the queue, message date, message time, symbolic source, text length, end key, status key and message count associated with an input message to be obtained with the RECEIVE and ACCEPT MESSAGE COUNT statements.

The CD entry is followed by one or more 01 record description entries which must contain exactly 87 characters which implicitly redefine the record area established by the CD entry. The 01 entry is divided in the following way:-

DATA DIVISION   COMMUNICATION SECTION cont.

COMMENTS cont.

Character Positions   Use

1-12   alphanumeric   Symbolic queue - gives the
                            symbolic message queue from
                            which the message is to be
                            received.

49-54 integer   Represents the date message
                            received in the form YYMMDD.

55-62 integer   Represents the time message
                            received in the form of
                            HHMMSSTT where TT is hundredths
                            of a second.

63-74 alphanumeric   Represents the symbolic name of
                            the terminal that is the source
                            of the message.

75-78 integer   Represents the number of
                            characters input as a result of
                            each RECEIVE statement.

79   alphanumeric   Represents a key which is set
                            to 3 when the end of a message
                            group is detected and to 2 when
                            the end of a message is
                            detected.

80-81 alphanumeric   Represents a status key with
                            the following meanings:

                                00-No error
                                20-Specified queue unknown
                                21-Symbolic source unknown

82-87 integer   Represents the number of
                            messages in existence in a
                            particular message queue and is
                            only updated by the ACCEPT
                            MESSAGE COUNT statement.

Fields 13-48 are not used in this level-1 feature.

The RECEIVE statement in the Procedure Division is
associated with this format and directs where the
incoming message is to be placed. See Page 145. See
also ACCEPT MESSAGE COUNT statement.

DATA DIVISION   **COMMUNICATION SECTION cont.**

COMMENTS cont.

Format 2.

This CD entry specifies the destination count, text length, status key, error key and symbolic destination of an output message associated with the SEND statement.

The CD entry is followed by one or more 01 record description entries which implicitly redefine the record area established by the output CD entry. The 01 record areas must be of 23 contiguous characters divided as explained below.

Character Position		Use
1-4	integer	Represents to the MCS the number of symbolic destinations that are to be used and in the level 1 Communications Feature should always be set to 1.
5-8	integer	Represents the text length to be output for each SEND statement.
9-10	alphanumeric	Represents a status key with the following meanings: 00-No error 10-Destination has been disabled 20-Destination unknown 30-Destination count invalid 50-Text length overflow 65-Output queue capacity exceeded
11	alphanumeric	Represents a key which will contain one of the following values after a SEND statement has been executed. 0-No error 1-Destination unknown 2-Destination has been disabled 6-Output queue capacity exceeded.

DATA DIVISION   COMMUNICATION SECTION cont.

COMMENTS cont.

Character Position   Use

  12-23 alphanumeric   Represents the symbolic destina-
                                 tion name of the recipient
                                 device.

The SEND statement is associated with this format and
directs the output of messages to output queues. (See
Page 145).

Format 3.

This CD entry describes the message date, message time,
symbolic terminal, text length, end key and status key
associated with a message either input by a RECEIVE
statement or output with a SEND statement.

The CD entry is followed by one or more 01 record
description entries which must contain exactly 33
characters which implicitly redefine the record area
established by the CD entry. The 01 entry is divided
in the following way.

Character Position   Use

  1-6   integer   Represents the date the message
                                 is sent in the form YYMMDD.

  7-14   integer   Represents the time the message
                                 is sent in the form HHMMSSTT
                                 where TT is hundredths of a
                                 second.

  15-26 alphanumeric   Represents the symbolic name of
                                 the sending or receiving
                                 terminal.

  27-30 integer   Represents the number of message
                                 characters to be transferred.

  31   alphanumeric   Represents a key set only by the
                                 RECEIVE statement with the
                                 following values:

                                   3-End of message group
                                   2-End of message
                                   0-Partial message transferred.

DATA DIVISION   **COMMUNICATION SECTION cont.**

COMMENTS cont.

<u>Character Position</u>   <u>Use</u>

  32-33 alphanumeric   Represents a status key having
                               values as described in format 1
                               and format 2 for RECEIVE and SEND
                               respectively.

This input-output format is used in association with the RECEIVE and SEND statements in the Procedure Division. (See Page 145).

DATA DIVISION COMMUNICATION SECTION cont.

EXAMPLES.

Format 1.

```
        .
    WORKING-STORAGE SECTION.
        .
    01  MSG-FLD             PIC X(100).
        .
    COMMUNICATION SECTION.
    CD  INPUT-DESC FOR INPUT
        QUEUE IS FLD-A
        MESSAGE DATE IS FLD-B
        MESSAGE TIME IS FLD-C
        SOURCE IS FLD-D
        TEXT LENGTH IS FLD-E
        END KEY IS FLD-F
        STATUS KEY IS FLD-G
        COUNT IS FLD-H.
    01  IN-REC.
        03  FLD-A      PIC X(12)   VALUE "MSG-QUEUE-1A".
        03  FILLER     PIC X(36).
        03  FLD-B      PIC 9(6).
        03  FLD-C      PIC 9(8).
        03  FLD-D      PIC X(12).
        03  FLD-E      PIC 9(4).
        03  FLD-F      PIC X.
        03  FLD-G      PIC XX.
        03  FLD-H      PIC 9(6).

    PROCEDURE DIVISION.
            .
            .
        RECEIVE INPUT-DESC MESSAGE INTO MSG-FLD.
            .
        ACCEPT INPUT-DESC MESSAGE COUNT.
        IF FLD-H = 500 PERFORM ROUTINE-1.
```

Format 2.

```
        .
    WORKING STORAGE SECTION.
        .
    01  MSG-FLD             PIC X(100).
        .
    COMMUNICATION SECTION.
```

DATA DIVISION   **COMMUNICATION SECTION cont.**

EXAMPLES cont.

-
    ```
    CD  OUTPUT-DESC FOR OUTPUT
        TEXT LENGTH IS MSG-SIZE
        SYMBOLIC DESTINATION IS DEST.
    01  OUT-REC.
        03 FILLER               PIC X(8).
        03 KEY-VAL              PIC XX.
            88 VAL-A    VALUE "00".
            88 VAL-B    VALUE "10".
            88 VAL-C    VALUE "20".
            88 VAL-D    VALUE "30".
            88 VAL-E    VALUE "50".
            88 VAL-F    VALUE "65".
        03 FILLER               PIC X(13).
    ```
-
    ```
    PROCEDURE DIVISION.
    ```
-
    ```
        MOVE 100 TO MSG-SIZE.
        MOVE SYMB-NAM TO DEST.
        SENT OUTPUT-DESC FROM MSG-FLD.
        IF NOT VAL-A PERFORM CHECK-ERR.
    ```
-

Format 3.
-
    ```
    WORKING-STORAGE SECTION.
    01  MSG-FLD             PIC X(50).
    ```
-
    ```
    COMMUNICATION SECTION.
    CD  I-O-DESC FOR I-O
        TERMINAL IS T-NAME
        TEXT LENGTH IS T-LENGTH.
    ```
-
    ```
    PROCEDURE DIVISION.
    ```
-
    ```
        SEND I-O-DESC FROM MSG-FLD.
    ```
-

NOTES.

DATA DIVISION   **REPORT SECTION**

FORMAT.

[REPORT SECTION.

 [RD report-name [CODE literal-1]

  [{CONTROLS ARE} {data-name-1 [data-name-2]...   }]
  [{CONTROL IS } {FINAL data-name-1 [data-name-2]...}]

    [PAGE [LIMIT IS] integer-1 [LINE] HEADING integer-2]
          [LIMITS ARE]   [LINES]

     [FIRST DETAIL integer-3]

     [LAST DETAIL   integer-4]

     [FOOTING   integer-5].

  {report-group-description entry}...]...]

COMMENTS.

The REPORT SECTION contains the report description entries used in conjunction with the Report Writer capabilities of COBOL. This section defines the report layout and control breaks of the reports generated by the Report Writer.

There must be an RD entry associated with each REPORT clause specified in any FD statements described in the File Section. The report-name given in the RD statement must be exactly the same as that given in the REPORT clause.

The CODE clause is used to specify an identifying character to be printed at the beginning of each line produced. This identification is meaningful when more than one report is produced.

The CONTROL clause is used to define the control breaks. The major control break is defined first and the least significant last. The FINAL clause is used for the control break which occurs at the end of a report.

The PAGE LIMIT clause gives the number of lines before page throw.

DATA DIVISION   **REPORT SECTION cont.**

COMMENTS cont.

The HEADING clause specifies the line number on which the first heading is to be printed. FIRST DETAIL gives the line number on which the first detail line may be printed, and LAST DETAIL gives the last line of detail print. FOOTING specifies the last CONTROL FOOTING print line, (PAGE FOOTING print lines are printed below integer-5 as far as the page limit specified by integer-1).

The RD entry is followed by the 01 report-group-description entries which are described in detail on pages 61 to 65. These entries have several special Report Writer functions. They can be given a TYPE, which means lines may be designated as heading, detail or footing (total) lines. The carriage control is indicated in the report-group-description using the LINE clause. The spacing of entries on a line is controlled using the COLUMN clause, and the particular entry is inserted in that position using the SOURCE clause. Totals can be accumulated using the SUM clause.

There are four Procedure Division verbs used with the Report Writer, INITIATE, GENERATE, SUPPRESS and TERMINATE which are fully described under the Procedure Division entries. INITIATE prepares for the report production. GENERATE deals with the printing of the lines. TERMINATE completes the processing of a report, and SUPPRESS inhibits report group printing.

EXAMPLE.

This example shows how to produce a report of the format below from a sequential disk file containing payroll details.

```
                       PAYROLL ANALYSIS
     DEPT     PAYROLL NO.     NAME           GROSS PAY
     01       1000            A SMITH         120.00
     01       1010            F JONES         130.00
     01       1300            I GREEN         115.00
                        DEPARTMENT TOTAL      365.00
     02       1200            C RILEY         100.00
      .         .               .               .
      .         .               .               .
      .         .               .               .
                         GRAND TOTAL        16100.00
```

DATA DIVISION   **REPORT SECTION cont.**

EXAMPLE cont.

```
   .
   .
FILE SECTION.
FD PAY-FILE       LABEL RECORDS OMITTED.
01 PAY-REC.
   03 DEPT                PIC 9(3).
   03 PAY-NO              PIC 9(4).
   03 NAME                PIC X(15).
   03 G-PAY               PIC 9(3)V99.
   .
FD PRINT-FILE LABEL RECORDS OMITTED
              REPORT IS PAY-REPORT.
   .
REPORT SECTION.
RD PAY-REPORT CONTROLS ARE FINAL, DEPT
              PAGE LIMIT IS 50 LINES.
01 TYPE PAGE HEADING.
   03 LINE 1.
      05 COLUMN 24 PIC X(16) VALUE "PAYROLL ANALYSIS".
   03 LINE PLUS 1.
      05 COLUMN  5 PIC X(49) VALUE
   "DEPT      PAYROLL NO.    NAME           GROSS PAY".
01 PAY-LINE TYPE DETAIL LINE PLUS 1.
   03 COLUMN  5    PIC 99 SOURCE DEPT.
   03 COLUMN 14    PIC 9(4) SOURCE PAY-NO.
   03 COLUMN 29    PIC X(15) SOURCE NAME.
   03 COLUMN 45    PIC ZZ9.99 SOURCE G-PAY.
01 TYPE CONTROL FOOTING, DEPT, LINE PLUS 1.
   03 COLUMN 21    PIC X(18) VALUE
                              "DEPARTMENTAL TOTAL".
   03 COLUMN 44    PIC ZZZ9.99 SOURCE SUM G-PAY.
01 TYPE CONTROL FOOTING, FINAL, LINE PLUS 1.
   03 COLUMN 21    PIC X(11) VALUE "GRAND TOTAL".
   03 COLUMN 43    PIC ZZZZ9.99 SOURCE SUM G-PAY.
   .
   .
```

DATA DIVISION   **REPORT SECTION cont.**

EXAMPLE cont.
   •
   •
   PROCEDURE DIVISION.
   •
   •
       OPEN INPUT PAY-FILE
            OUTPUT PRINT-FILE.
       INITIATE PAY-REPORT.
   READ-FILE.
       READ PAY-FILE AT END GO TO END-REPORT.
       GENERATE PAY-LINE.
       GO TO READ-FILE.
   END-REPORT.
       TERMINATE PAY-REPORT.
       CLOSE PAY-FILE
             PRINT-FILE.
   •
       STOP RUN.

NOTES.

DATA DIVISION   Data Description Entries

FORMAT 1.

    level-number { data-name-1 } clause
                         { FILLER   }

       [REDEFINES clause]

       [BLANK when ZERO clause]

       [JUSTIFIED clause]

       [OCCURS clause]

       [PICTURE clause]

       [SIGN clause]

       [SYNCHRONIZED clause]

       [USAGE clause]

       [VALUE clause]

FORMAT 2.

    66   data-name RENAMES clause

FORMAT 3.

    88   condition-name VALUE clause

COMMENTS.

Format 1 is used for all record descriptions entries in the Data Division, and for Level-77 entries in the Working-Storage and Linkage Sections. This entry is used subject to the following formation rules.

- level number may be any number from 01 to 49 or 77.

- the clauses may be written in any order, except that the data-name (or FILLER) must immediately follow the level number, and when the REDEFINES clause is specified it must immediately follow the data name clause.

- the PICTURE clause must be specified for every elementary item except indexed data items (see

DATA DIVISION   Data Description Entries cont.

COMMENTS cont.

    OCCURS, Page 72).

- the BLANK WHEN ZERO, JUSTIFIED, PICTURE and SYNCHRONIZED clauses must only be specified for elementary items.

- a space, comma or semicolon must seperate clauses.

- each entry must be terminated by a period.

Format 2, the level-66 entry, is used to rename, or regroup, previously defined data items. Level-66 entries are defined in detail on Page 92.

Format 3, the level-88 entry, is used to assign a testable condition name to certain values which may be found in a data item. It is described in detail on Page 93.

The various clauses associated with the Format 1 entry are described on the following pages.

EXAMPLES.

```
01  RECORD-ENTRY.
    03 TYPE-A       PICTURE X(4).
    03 TYPE-B REDEFINES TYPE-A   PIC 9(4).
    03 TYPE-C       PIC 9(8)V99 BLANK WHEN ZERO.
    03 TYPE-D       PIC A(4) JUSTIFIED RIGHT.
    03 TYPE-E       PIC X    OCCURS 3 TIMES.
    03 TYPE-F       PIC S99  SIGN IS LEADING.
    03 TYPE-G       PIC S9(8) COMP SYNC.
    03 TYPE-H       PIC X(4) USAGE IS DISPLAY.
    03 TYPE-I       PIC X(3) VALUE "ABC".
    03 SUB-GROUP.
       05 FILLER    PIC X(15).
       05 NME       PIC X(15).
```

DATA DIVISION   Data Description Entries cont.

EXAMPLES cont.

```
77 HOLD-FLD                   PIC X(5).

77 COUNTER                    PIC 9(5) VALUE ZERO.

01 GRP-1.
   03 FLD-1                   PIC XXX.
   03 FLD-2                   PIC XXX.
   03 FLD-3                   PIC XXX.
66 FLD-REN RENAMES FLD2 THRU FLD-3.

01 PET ENTRY.
   03 NAME                    PIC X(9).
   03 PET-CODE                PIC X.
      88 DOG                  VALUE "D".
      88 CAT                  VALUE "C".
      88 RAT                  VALUE "R".


77 MNTH                       PIC 99.
   88 SUMMER                  VALUE 6 THRU 9.
```

NOTES.

DATA DIVISION   Report Group Description Entries

FORMAT 1.

```
01 [data-name-1]
```

   [LINE NUMBER IS {Integer-1 ON NEXT PAGE / PLUS integer-2}]

   [NEXT GROUP IS {integer-3 / PLUS integer-4 / NEXT PAGE}]

   TYPE IS {
       {REPORT HEADING / RH}
       {PAGE HEADING / PH}
       {CONTROL HEADING / CH} {data-name-2 / FINAL}
       {DETAIL / DE}
       {CONTROL FOOTING / CF} {data-name-3 / FINAL}
       {PAGE FOOTING / PF}
       {REPORT FOOTING / RF}
   }

   [[USAGE IS] DISPLAY].

FORMAT 2.

```
level-number [data-name-1]
```

   LINE NUMBER IS {integer-1 ON NEXT PAGE / PLUS integer-2}

   [[USAGE IS] DISPLAY].

DATA DIVISION   Report Group Description Entries cont.

FORMAT 3.

  Level-number [data-name-1]

    [BLANK WHEN ZERO]

    [COLUMN NUMBER IS integer-1]

    [GROUP INDICATE]

    [{JUSTIFIED / JUST} RIGHT]

    [LINE NUMBER IS {integer-1 ON NEXT PAGE / PLUS integer-2}]

    {PICTURE / PIC} IS character-string

    {
      SOURCE IS identifier-1
      VALUE IS literal-1
      {SUM identifier-2 [identifier-3]...
        [UPON data-name-2 [data-name-3]...]}...
        [RESET ON {data-name-4 / FINAL}]
    }

    [[USAGE IS] DISPLAY].

COMMENTS.

The Report Group Description entries are used to describe the format of a report group as produced by the Report Writer capability of COBOL.

These entries follow the Report Description entry (RD) in the Report Section. The RD entry describes the overall physical aspects of the report, whilst the Report Group Description entries describe the characteristics of each report group within the report. The RD entry is described in detail on Page 54 and should be referred to in conjunction with the entry described here

DATA DIVISION   Report Group Description Entries cont.

COMMENTS cont.

The report generated by the Report Writer function consists of one or more report groups. There are 3 basic types of report groups; heading groups, detail groups and footing groups.

Format 1 is used to describe a level 01 report group entry. Each report group must contain a level 01 entry of this kind, and it must be the first entry.

Format 2 is used to describe a group item which may have a level number of 02 through 48. It is used to specify the line number of subordinate items and to group elementary items together.

Format 3 is used to describe an elementary entry which may have level number of 01 through 49. If a level 01 elementary item is specified then the report group consists of only one elementary item, and this must be the only entry for the report group. Format 3 entries describe the precise position, characteristics and content of each elementary item printed by the report.

The following is a description of each of the clauses specified in the above formats.

<u>LINE</u> clause.

This clause gives the line number of the entry either absolute from the page beginning, or relative from the previous line. The NEXT PAGE option indicates on which line, after page throw, the printing is to take place. The PLUS option indicates how many lines to skip from the previous printed line. Each line in a report must have an associated LINE clause.

<u>NEXT GROUP</u> clause.

This clause specifies the spacing between two report groups. Integer-3 indicates the line number on the current page at which the next report group will begin. The PLUS option indicates the number of lines from the last line of the previous group at which printing of the new group is to begin. NEXT PAGE indicates that the printing of the new group will begin on the next page.

DATA DIVISION   Report Group Description Entries cont.

COMMENTS cont.

TYPE clause.

The TYPE clause specifies the type of report group to be generated. REPORT HEADING indicates that the group specified is to be printed at the beginning of the report only.
PAGE HEADING indicates printing only at the heading of each page.
CONTROL HEADING indicates printing at the control break produced by a change of the contents of data-name-2, or in the case of FINAL, at the end of the report.
DETAIL indicates printing for each detail line upon encountering each GENERATE statement in the Procedure Division.
CONTROL FOOTING indicates printing at the end of each control group as specified by data-name-3 or in the case of FINAL, at the end of report.
PAGE FOOTING indicates a report group printed at the bottom of each page.
REPORT FOOTING indicates a report group printed at the termination of a report.

USAGE clause.

Each elementary report entry must have a USAGE DISPLAY either explicitly defined using this clause or implicitly defined by the default.

BLANK WHEN ZERO clause.

This clause is described on page 70.

COLUMN clause.

This clause indicates the column position of the leftmost character of an elementary item.

GROUP INDICATE clause.

This clause indicates that the elementary item is only to be produced the first time a control or page break occurs. It is not produced upon any subsequent breaks.

JUSTIFIED clause.

This clause is described on Page 71.

DATA DIVISION   Report Group Description Entries cont.

COMMENTS cont.

PICTURE clause.

This clause is described on Page 75.

SOURCE clause.

This clause specifies the identifier which is to be used to give a value to the elementary item to be printed. The identifier must be a data item defined outside the Report Section, or the name of a SUM counter.

VALUE clause.

This clause is used to give an elementary printed item a certain value, which must conform to the item's PICTURE clause. The item is given this value each time the report group is produced.

SUM clause.

This clause is used to designate an elementary item as the receiving field for a series of summations on SOURCE data items. This clause can only be used within a CONTROL FOOTING report group. The UPON option allows two or more named source items to be summed into one data item. The RESET option specifies when a sum counter may be reset to zero after a control break, or the FINAL control break.

The Procedure Division considerations for the Report Writer are detailed on Page 120.

EXAMPLE.

Examples of the Report Writer are given on Pages 55 and 121.

NOTES.

DATA DIVISION   **Level Numbers**

Level numbers are used to specify the hierarchical relationships of data items. There are also some special data items with certain functions. The allowable level numbers and their uses are described below:

Level number   Use

   01   Indicates the highest level in a data hierarchy, such as a record. It may be a group item or an elementary item. For coding purposes the 01 always begins in Area A (columns 8,9,10 or 11).

   02-49   Indicates the levels subordinate to the 01 level. Items with these levels may again be elementary or may be grouped. Subordinate members of a group must have level numbers higher than that of the group item itself. These level numbers must be coded in, or to the right of column 12.

   66   Indicates a name which RENAMES an item or set of items (see Page 92).

   77   Indicates an independent Working-Storage or Linkage Section data item. It must begin in Area A.

   88   Indicates a condition name which may be given to certain values held in a data item.

EXAMPLES.

```
   01  GROUP-FIELD.
       03  NAME.
           05  INIT        PIC XX.
           05  SURN        PIC X(15).
       03  DOB             PIC X(8).

   01  TOT-REC             PIC X(80).

   77  COUNT-FLD           PIC 999.
```

NOTES.

DATA DIVISION   data-name/FILLER

FORMAT.

$$\begin{Bmatrix} \text{data-name} \\ \text{FILLER} \end{Bmatrix}$$

COMMENTS.

The data-name specifies the name of the data being described, and the word FILLER refers to an elementary item that does not need to be referred to explicitly.

In the File, Working-Storage, Communication and Linkage Sections a data-name or a FILLER must be the first word immediately following the level number in each data description.

The data-name is a user-defined word and must be not more than 30 characters long, and may be made up of the characters A to Z, 0 to 9 and - , although - may not appear as the first or last character.

EXAMPLES.

```
    01  REC-1.
        03  ITEM-A        PIC X(6)    VALUE "AMOUNT".
        03  FILLER        PIC X(4)    VALUE SPACES.
        03  ITEM-B        PIC 9(4).99
        03  FILLER        PIC X(4)    VALUE SPACES.
```

NOTES.

DATA DIVISION   REDEFINES

FORMAT.

    level-number data-name-1 REDEFINES data-name-2

COMMENTS.

The REDEFINES clause allows the same storage area to contain different data items. That is, it allows a defined storage area to be redefined as an area of different characteristics.

The level numbers of the two data items must be the same, and may not be level 66 or level 88.

The data description entry for data-name-2 may not contain an OCCURS clause, although an OCCURS may be specified for an item which has data-name-2 as a subordinate.

The redefinition of data-name-2 begins at data-name-1 and ends when a level number less than or equal to that of data-name-2 is encountered.

When more than one level 01 entry is associated with a FD or SD entry then implicit redefinition of the first 01 area is assumed.

The redefined item and the redefining item must be of the same size. The redefining entry and any subordinate entries may not contain the VALUE clause, although they may have a different usage.

Multiple redefining is allowed, provided the redefining items immediately follow the original entry and all use the data-name of the original entry.

EXAMPLES.

```
   .
   .
   03 FIELD-A                            PIC X(6).
   03 FIELD-B REDEFINES FIELD-A          PIC 9(4)V99.
   .
```

DATA DIVISION   **REDEFINES cont.**

EXAMPLES cont.

-
```
01 REC-1.
   03 PART-NO                                 PIC X(6).
   03 PART-DESC                               PIC X(25).
   03 IN-OUT                                  PIC X.
   03 SOURCE-CODE.
      03 SITE                                 PIC XX.
      03 DATE-S                               PIC 9(6).
   03 DEST-CODE REDEFINES SOURCE-CODE         PIC X(8).
```
-
-
```
   03 A              PIC XX.
   03 B REDEFINES A  PIC 99.
   03 C REDEFINES A  PIC AA.
```
-
-
```
01 SEASONS-TABLE.
   03 CONTENTS.
      05 WINT      PIC X(6) VALUE "WINTER".
      05 SPRI      PIC X(6) VALUE "SPRING".
      05 SUMM      PIC X(6) VALUE "SUMMER".
      05 AUTU      PIC X(6) VALUE "AUTUMN".
   03 FILLER REDEFINES CONTENTS.
      05 SEASON OCCURS 4 TIMES    PIC X(6).
```
-
-

NOTES.

DATA DIVISION   BLANK WHEN ZERO

FORMAT.

    <u>BLANK</u> WHEN <u>ZERO</u>

COMMENTS.

The BLANK WHEN ZERO clause specifies that when the
associated data item has the value zero it is then
filled with spaces. This clause may only be specified
for elementary numeric or numeric edited items. When
it is specified for a purely numeric item, that item is
considered to be numeric edited.

The BLANK WHEN ZERO clause must not be specified for
level 66 or level 88 items.

EXAMPLE.

```
         .
         .
         01  REC-O.
             03 NAM-O           PIC X(10).
             03 FILLER          PIC X(5) VALUE SPACES.
             03 ADD-O           PIC X(30).
             03 FILLER          PIC X(5) VALUE SPACES.
             03 COST-O          PIC 99.99 BLANK WHEN ZERO.
             03 FILLER          PIC X(5) VALUE SPACES.
```

NOTES.

DATA DIVISION   **JUSTIFIED**

FORMAT.

$$\left\{ \begin{array}{l} \underline{\text{JUSTIFIED}} \\ \underline{\text{JUST}} \end{array} \right\} \quad \text{RIGHT}$$

COMMENTS.

The JUSTIFIED clause is used to override the normal left justification of received alphabetic or alphanumeric data items. The data becomes aligned on the rightmost character position of the receiving items.

JUSTIFIED may only be specified for elementary non-edited alphanumeric items and alphabetic items.

When the sending item is larger than the receiving justified item then left truncation occurs, and when the sending item is smaller left-most space fill occurs.

EXAMPLES.

```
   .
   .
   77 FIELD-A            PIC X(4)   VALUE "AB  ".
   .
   77 FIELD-B            PIC X(6)   JUSTIFIED RIGHT.
   .
   PROCEDURE DIVISION.

       MOVE FIELD-A TO FIELD-B.
   .
```

As a result of this move FIELD-B would contain "   AB".

NOTES.

DATA DIVISION   OCCURS

FORMAT.

   [OCCURS $\left\{ \begin{array}{l} \text{integer-1 } \underline{\text{TO}} \text{ integer-2 TIMES} \\ \text{integer-3 } \underline{\text{TIMES}} \end{array} \right.$ $\left. \begin{array}{l} \underline{\text{DEPENDING}} \text{ ON} \\ \text{data-name-1} \end{array} \right\}$

   [$\left\{ \begin{array}{l} \underline{\text{ASCENDING}} \\ \underline{\text{DESCENDING}} \end{array} \right\}$ KEY IS data-name-2 [data-name-3]...]...

           [<u>INDEXED</u> BY index-name-1 [index-name-2]...]]

COMMENTS.

The OCCURS clause is used to specify a data item which may be repeated to form a table. The table entries may be accessed using subscripts or indices.

The OCCURS clause may not be specified for 01, 66, 77 or 88 level entries.

The OCCURS integer-3 TIMES will create a table of integer-3 entries. The OCCURS DEPENDING ON option allows the table to have a variable size during program execution. Integer-1 represents the minimum table size, integer-2 represents the maximum table size, and data-name-1 contains positive integer which is the number of table elements.

The KEY IS option specifies that the repeated data is arranged in ascending or descending order upon the key specified in order of significance by data-name-2, data-name-3 etc. It is the responsibility of the programmer to ensure the entries are in the specified order. The ascending or descending key items are used in the SEARCH ALL non-serial (binary) table search.

The INDEXED BY option specifies that indices may be used with the table elements. The index is a compiler-generated storage area used to store table element occurence numbers, and contains a binary value that represents a displacement from the beginning of the table element. There are two methods of indexing. In direct indexing the index-name is used in the form of a subscript. Relative indexing is specified when the index-name is followed by the operator + or -, followed by an unsigned integer.

DATA DIVISION   **OCCURS cont.**

COMMENTS cont.

When the subject of an OCCURS clause is a group item, then the group item itself, or items subordinate to it, must be subscripted or indexed.

EXAMPLES.

```
   01 NAME-LIST.
      03   NAME-TAB      OCCURS 10 TIMES      PIC X(5).

   01 PART-LIST.
      03   PART-TAB      OCCURS 100 TIMES.
           05 PART-NO                         PIC X(50).
           05 PART-NAM                        PIC X(10).

   01 GROUP-TAB.
      03   TAB-CONT.
           05 D1         PIC X(3) VALUE "SUN".
           05 D2         PIC X(3) VALUE "MON".
           05 D3         PIC X(3) VALUE "TUE".
           05 D4         PIC X(3) VALUE "WED".
           05 D5         PIC X(3) VALUE "THU".
           05 D6         PIC X(3) VALUE "FRI".
           05 D7         PIC X(3) VALUE "SAT".
      03   TAB-ENT REDEFINES TAB-CONT.
           05 DAY-IS OCCURS 7 TIMES   PIC XXX.

   01 TABLE-2D.
      03   ELEMENT-1 OCCURS 10 TIMES.
           05 ELEMENT-2 OCCURS 10 TIMES.
              07 A       PIC X(5).
              07 B       PIC 9(5).

   01 EMP-TAB.
      03   EMP-REC   OCCURS 100 TIMES ASCENDING KEY
                                       IS EMP-NO.
           05 EMP-NO    PIC 9(5).
           05 EMP-NAM   PIC X(15).
```

DATA DIVISION **OCCURS cont.**

EXAMPLES cont.

-
```
01 INDEXED-TAB.
   03 IND-TAB OCCURS 100 TIMES ASCENDING KEY IS
                    FIELD-1 INDEXED BY INDEX-A.
      05 FIELD-1         PIC 9(4).
      05 FIELD-2         PIC X(10).
      05 FIELD-3         PIC X(10).
```
-
-
```
77 SUB1                  PIC 99.
77 SUB2                  PIC 999.
77 SUB3                  PIC 9 VALUE 1.
77 SUB5                  PIC 999.
```
-
```
PROCEDURE DIVISION.
```
-
```
   MOVE 1 TO SUB1.
   MOVE NAM-IN TO NAME-TAB (SUB1).
```
-
```
   ADD 1 TO SUB2.
   IF PART-NO (SUB2) = "99999" GO TO ERR-ROUT.
```
-
```
   IF DAY-IS (SUB3) = "SUN" DISPLAY "START THE WEEK".
```
-
```
   MOVE ELEMENT-2 (1,1) TO OUTPUT-2.
```
-
```
   MOVE ZERO TO IND-TAB (INDEX-A).
```
-
```
   MOVE ZERO TO IND-TAB (INDEX-A + 1).
```

NOTES.

DATA DIVISION **PICTURE**

FORMAT.

    level-number {data-name} {PICTURE} IS character-string
                             {FILLER}   {PIC}

COMMENTS.

The PICTURE clause is used to describe the characteristics of an elementary item. The PICTURE clause may only be specified at an elementary level.

The character string may be up to 30 characters in length.

Symbols used in the PICTURE clause:

Character   **Use**

    A   Represents a character position for an alphabetic character or space.

    B   Represents the character position for a space.

    P   Represents the position of an assumed decimal point when that point is not within the number contained in the data item. The scaling position character P is not counted in the size of the data item. For example, PIC PP99 defines a two character numeric item whose range is .0001 through .0099, or zero.

                    The character P may only appear to the left or right of other characters in the string as a continuous string of P's. The picture character S and V are the only ones which may appear to the left of a string of P's. For example, PIC 9V9PP defines a two character numeric item whose range is 0.000 through 9.900.

    S   Represents the presence of an operational sign. It must be written as the leftmost character of the PICTURE string. The S symbol is not counted in the size of the elementary item, unless the SIGN clause with seperate character has been used.

DATA DIVISION   **PICTURE cont.**

COMMENTS cont.

Character   Use

V	Represents an assumed decimal point. It does not count in the size of the elementary item, and only one may occur in any string.
X	Represents the position of an alphanumeric character.
Z	Represents a zero suppression character. Whenever that position contains a zero, it is replaced by a space. Z characters are counted in the size of the item.
9	Represents the position of a numeric character.
0	Represents the position where the numeral zero will be inserted into the character string.
/	Represents the position where the stroke character will be inserted into the character string.
,	Represents the position where the comma character will be inserted into the character string.
.	Represents the position where a decimal point is to be inserted and the source item is aligned accordingly.
*	Represents a zero replacement character. Whenever the character position contains a zero, and it is on the left of the most significant non-zero digit, it is replaced by an asterisk.
$	Represents the position where the currency sign will be inserted.
CR DB	Represents the position where a CR or DB will be inserted if the source item is negative. Spaces are inserted if it is positive. These characters are counted in the size of the item.

DATA DIVISION   **PICTURE cont.**

COMMENTS cont.

Character   **Use**

   + -   Represent the position where a sign may be
                  printed. If a + is used then a plus
                  symbol is printed for positive or zero
                  values, and a minus symbol for negative
                  values. If a - is used, then a minus
                  symbol is inserted for negative values,
                  and a space for positive or zero values.

The symbols CR, DB, + and - are all mutually exclusive
in a character string, and they do count towards the
size of the item.

Certain symbols, if they are followed by an integer in
parentheses, are repeated by that integer number of
times. For example, PIC 9(5) is the equivalent of PIC
99999. Allowable repetition symbols are:

                A , X 9 P Z * B 0 - $

The following is a description of valid PICTURE usage
for the five categories of data.

1. <u>Alphabetic items.</u>

   An alphabetic item is one where PICTURE string
   contains only the character A. The contents of the
   field may only be made up of the 26 letters of the
   alphabet and the space character.

2. <u>Alphanumeric items.</u>

   The PICTURE string of an alphanumeric item may only
   contain the symbols A X and 9. The field may
   contain any character out of the computer's
   character set.

3. <u>Numeric items.</u>

   The PICTURE string of a numeric item may only
   contain the symbols 9 V P and S. The field may
   contain any combination of the numbers 0 to 9 and an
   operational sign. The V, when present indicates the
   position of an assumed decimal point. The maximum
   size of a numeric item is 18 digits.

   The USAGE of the item may be DISPLAY or COMPUTATIONAL.

DATA DIVISION   PICTURE cont.

COMMENTS cont.

4. <u>Alphabetic Edited items</u>.

   An alphanumeric edited item has a PICTURE string made up of combinations of the following symbols.

           A X 9 B 0 /

   To be considered alphanumeric edited the string must contain at least one of the combinations of a least:
           -one B and one X
           -one 0 and one X
           -one / and one X
           -one 0 and one A
           -one / and one A

   The contents of the item, in standard form, may be anything from the computer's character set.

5. <u>Numeric Edited items</u>.

   A numeric edited item is one whose PICTURE string may contain certain combinations of the following symbols:

           B P V Z 0 9 , * = - CR DB $

   The maximum number of digit positions is 18 and the maximum length of a numeric edited item is 128 characters.

   The allowable combinations of symbols are defined by the PICTURE Symbol Order Table (Page 83) and the editing rules.

<u>PICTURE clause editing</u>.

   There are two basic types of editing:

       - Insertion editing

       - Suppression and replacement editing

DATA DIVISION   **PICTURE cont.**

COMMENTS cont.

Insertion editing.

There are four types of insertion editing.

a. Simple insertion editing using the characters B 0 / and , (comma) subject to the following category rules.

Category	Valid Insertion Symbols
Alphabetic	B
Alphanumeric edited	B 0 /
Numeric edited	b 0 / ,

b. Special insertion editing using the period (.) as the insertion character. The period represents the actual position of the decimal point, and is also used for alignment purposes. This is only valid for numeric edited items.

c. Fixed insertion editing using the symbols CR DB + and -. This type of editing can only be carried out for numeric edited items.

d. Floating insertion editing using the symbols $ + and -. This is only valid for numeric edited items and involves the floating of the editing symbol to the start of the significance of the item being edited. See examples.

To avoid the danger of truncation in floating insertion editing the minimum size of the PICTURE character string must be the sum the number of characters in the sending field, the number of non-floating insertion symbols in the receiving field, and one character for the floating insertion symbol.

DATA DIVISION   PICTURE cont.

COMMENTS cont.

    ZERO Suppression and Replacement Editing.

    This type of editing is only valid for numeric edited items, and involves the use of the Z and * symbols.

    This editing is carried out by using a string of Z or * symbols in the leftmost character positions of the PICTURE string. When the character positions to the left of significance are represented by a Z or * and contain zero, then that zero is replaced by a space (in the case of Z) or an * (in the case of *). See examples.

EXAMPLES.

Alphabetic item.

    77   ALPHAB   PIC A(5) VALUE " ABCD".

Alphanumeric items.

    01   ALPHAN-A   PIC X(5) VALUE " AB12".

    77   ALPHAN-B   PIC AAXX VALUE " AB12".

Numeric Items.

Picture	Valid range of values
99	0 through 99
S9V99	-9.99 through +9.99
PP999	0 through .00999
999PP	100 through 99900

DATA DIVISION   **PICTURE cont.**

EXAMPLES cont.

Simple insertion editing.

Picture	Value of Data	Edited Result	Type
AABAA	ABCD	AB CD	Alphab edited
XX/XX	1234	12/34	Alphanum edited
00XXX	123	00123	Alphanum edited
9,999	1234	1,234	Numeric edited
99900	123	12300	Numeric edited
9BB99	1234	2 34	Numeric edited

Special insertion editing.

Picture	Value of Data	Edited Result
99.99	1.23	01.23
99.99	1.234	01.23
99.99	12.34	12.34
99.99	123.4	23.40

Fixed insertion editing.

Picture	Value of Data	Edited Result
+99.99	+12.34	+12.34
+99.99	-12.34	-12.34
-99.99	-12.34	-12.34
-99.99	+12.34	12.34
-$99.99	-12.34	-$12.34
99.99CR	-12.34	12.34CR
99.99CR	+12.34	12.34
99.99DB	-12.34	12.34DB

Floating insertion editing.

Picture	Value of Data	Edited Result
$$$9.9	123.4	$123.4
$$99.9	.1	$00.1

| DATA DIVISION | PICTURE cont. |

EXAMPLES cont.

Floating insertion editing cont.

Picture	Value of Data	Edited Result
$,$$9.99	12.34	$12.34
++++9.99	-.12	-0.12
-,---.--	00.00	

Zero suppression and replacement editing.

Picture	Value of Data	Editing Result
***9.99	0000.12	***0.12
ZZZ9.99	0000.12	0.12
ZZZZ.ZZ	0000.00	
****.**	0000.00	****.**
$ZZZZ.ZZ	0001.23	$ 1.23
$ZZZ9.99CR	-.12	$ 0.12CR

NOTES.

DATA DIVISION   **PICTURE cont.**

PICTURE Character Precedence Chart. PART 1.

FIRST SYM. → ↓ SECOND SYM.	NON-FLOATING INSERTION SYMBOLS (NFIS) B O / , . {+/−} {+/−} {CR/DB} CS	FLOATING INSERTION SYMBOLS (FIS) {Z/*} {Z/*} {+/−} {+/−} CS CS	OTHER SYMBOLS 9 {A/X} S V P P
B	X X X X X X	X X X X X X	X X X X
0	X X X X X X	X X X X X X	X X X X
/	X X X X X X	X X X X X X	X X X X
,	X X X X X X	X X X X X X	X X X X
.	X X X X X	X X X X	X
NFIS {+/−}			
{+/−}	X X X X X X	X X X X	X X X X
{CR/DB}	X X X X X X	X X X X	X X X X
cs	X		

The chart on this and the following page illustrate the order of precedence when using characters in a PICTURE character string. An X at an intersection indicates that symbols at the top of the column may precede the symbols at the left of the row. The currency symbol is indicated by cs.

Some symbols appear twice. In this case the leftmost column and uppermost row indicate use of the symbol to the left of the decimal point, and rightmost and lower indicate usage to the right of the decimal point.

DATA DIVISION   **PICTURE cont.**

PICTURE Character Precedence Chart. PART 2.

FIRST SYM. → ↓ SECOND SYM.		NON-FLOATING INSERTION SYMBOLS (NFIS) B 0 / , . {+/-} {+/-}{CR/DB} cs	FLOATING INSERTION SYMBOLS (FIS) {Z/*} {Z/*} {+/-} {+/-} cs cs	OTHER SYMBOLS 9 {A/X} S V P P
FIS	{Z/*}	X X X X X X		
	{Z/*}	X X X X X X	X X	X X
	{+/-}	X X X X X	X	
	{+/-}	X X X X X	X X	X X
	cs	X X X X X	X	
	cs	X X X X X X	X X	X X
OTHER SYM.	9	X X X X X X	X X X	X X X X X
	{A/X}	X X X		X X
	S			
	V	X X X X X X	X X	X X X
	P	X X X X X X	X X	X X X
	P	X X		X X X

DATA DIVISION   **SIGN**

FORMAT.

```
[SIGN IS]   {LEADING }  [SEPERATE CHARACTER]
            {TRAILING}
```

COMMENTS.

The SIGN clause specifies the characteristics of the operational sign.

The clause may only be specified for an elementary item containing an S in its PICTURE, or for a group item containing one such elementary item. The item concerned must be specified as USAGE IS DISPLAY, either explicitly or implicitly.

If the SEPARATE CHARACTER option is omitted then the sign is associated with the LEADING or TRAILING character position, and the sign is not included in determining the size of the item.

If the SEPARATE CHARACTER option is included, then the sign is associated with the LEADING or TRAILING character position, and the sign is included in determining the size of the item. The sign, in this case, is always represented by the characters "+" or "-". If the CODE SET clause is specified for a file, then all signed numeric items in that file must use the SEPARATE CHARACTER option.

EXAMPLES.

```
    .
    01 REC-1
       03 NUM-1     PIC S99V99 SIGN IS LEADING SEPARATE
                                                CHARACTER.
    .
    FD FILE-1.
        .
        CODE SET IS ASCII-SEQUENCE.
    .
    01 FILE-1-REC.
        .
        03 REC-NUM    PIC S99 SIGN IS SEPARATE.
```

NOTES.

DATA DIVISION   SYNCHRONISED

FORMAT.

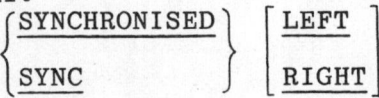

$$\begin{Bmatrix} \text{SYNCHRONISED} \\ \text{SYNC} \end{Bmatrix} \begin{bmatrix} \text{LEFT} \\ \text{RIGHT} \end{bmatrix}$$

COMMENTS.

The SYNCHRONISED clause specifies the alignment of elementary items upon storage boundaries as defined for the particular computer in use, (e.g. word boundaries, byte boundaries etc).

In general, within an object program, data items are placed without regard to storage boundaries. This may reduce access efficiency, but for items accessed infrequently this is not a major consideration. However, for items which are accessed frequently (e.g. accumulators used in iterative calculations) this can be a major efficiency consideration. For this reason the SYNCHRONISED clause can be used for boundary alignment.

When the SYNCHRONISED clause is used the data item is synchronised by leftmost, or rightmost, character on a proper boundary. Any character positions remaining between the end of the item and the next boundary may not be used for another data item. Such unused positions are, however, included in the size of a group item or for when the item is the object of a REDEFINES clause. These unused character positions are termed slack bytes.

If the RIGHT or LEFT options are omitted, then the synchronised position is implementor dependent.

When the SYNCHRONISED clause is associated with the OCCURS clause, then each repeated item is likewise synchronised.

DATA DIVISION   **SYNCHRONISED cont.**

EXAMPLES.

```
01  ACCUM-FLDS.
    03 ACCUM-1          PIC 9(3).
    03 FILLER           PIC X.
    03 ACCUM-2          PIC 9(4) SYNC LEFT.


01  OCCUR-REC.
    03 CODE-1           PIC X.
    03 TABLE-ENTRIES OCCURS 10 TIMES.
       05 SLACK-B       PIC X(3).
       05 ACCUM         PIC X(4) COMP SYNC.

01  RECORD-1.
    03 FIELD-1          PIC X(5).
    03 FIELD-2 REDEFINES FIELD-1.
       05 FILLER        PIC X.
       05 ARITH-AREA    PIC 9(3) SYNC RIGHT.
       05 FILLER        PIC X.
```

The above examples assume 4 byte boundaries.

NOTES.

DATA DIVISION   USAGE

FORMAT.

    [USAGE IS] { COMPUTATIONAL / COMP / DISPLAY / INDEX }

COMMENTS.

The USAGE clause specifies the format of the data item in storage.

It can be written for an item at any level, and if a group item is specified then the USAGE specified applies to all subordinate items.

The default usage for any item is DISPLAY. DISPLAY indicates that the format of the data is a standard data format.

USAGE IS COMPUTATIONAL (or COMP) indicates that the data item is held in a binary form. The PICTURE of such an item may only contain the characters 9, S, V and P.

The USAGE IS INDEX clause specifies that the data item concerned is to be used as an index data item. The item is used to store values equivalent to the occurrences of elements within a table, and will be used in association with the OCCURS clause and table handling.

The index data item can only be referred to explicitly by the SEARCH or SET statements, a relation condition, the USING phrase of a Procedure Division header, or the USING phrase of a CALL statement. The external or internal format of an index data item is implementor dependent.

DATA DIVISION   **USAGE cont.**

EXAMPLES.

```
                                          Example   Internal
01 EGS.                                   Value     Rep.
   03 D-1 PIC  9999 USAGE DISPLAY.         1234     F1 F2 F3 C4
   03 D-2 PIC S9999 USAGE DISPLAY.        +1234     F1 F2 F3 C4
   03 D-3 PIC S9999 USAGE DISPLAY.        -1234     F1 F2 F3 D4
   03
   03 COMP-1 PIC  9999 USAGE COMP.         1234     04 D2
   03 COMP-2 PIC S9999 USAGE COMP.        +1234     04 D2
   03 COMP-3 PIC S9999 USAGE COMP.        -1234     FB 2E

   03 IND              USAGE INDEX.
```

(The above examples use the EBCDIC code with two hexadecimal digits representing one byte. Negative numbers in the binary form are shown as 2's complement).

NOTES.

DATA DIVISION   VALUE

FORMAT.

  [<u>VALUE</u> IS literal]

COMMENTS.

The VALUE clause is used to specify the initial
contents of a data item or values of certain condition
names. Only the initialization feature is described
here. VALUE associated with condition names is
described on page 93.

The VALUE clause may be used in the Working-Storage and
Communication Sections to define initial values, and in
the Report Section to define the constant value of an
elementary report group item. It may not be used in
the File or Linkage Sections for initialization
purposes.

The literal given must conform to the PICTURE
characteristics of the data item. If the data is
numeric, then the literal must be numeric. If the item
is alphabetic, alphanumeric, alphanumeric-edited or
numeric edited, then the VALUE clause must describe a
non-numeric literal.

The literal may be substituted with an appropriate
figurative constant.

The VALUE clause may not be associated with an entry
which contains an OCCURS or REDEFINES clause, or for an
entry subordinate to an item containing an OCCURS or
REDEFINES clause.

The VALUE clause may be specified at group level
provided a figurative constant or nonnumeric literal is
used. The value clause may not then be used for
subordinate items to the group. Also a group item may
not have a VALUE clause if any subordinate items have
JUSTIFIED, SYNCHRONISED or USAGE (other than DISPLAY)
clauses.

DATA DIVISION   **VALUE cont.**

EXAMPLES.

```
    77 ITEM-1           PIC X(5) VALUE "AB 12".
    77 ITEM-2           PIC 9(8)V99 VALUE 123.4.
    77 ITEM-3           PIC S9(4) VALUE -0123.

    01 GROUP-A    VALUE SPACES.
       02 ITEM-4        PIC X(4).
       02 ITEM-5        PIC 9(4).
    01 ITEM-7           PIC 99PP VALUE 1000.
    01 ITEM-8           PIC PP99 VALUE .0001.

    01 AST-LINE         PIC X(123) VALUE ALL "*".
```

NOTES.

DATA DIVISION   Level 66 RENAMES

FORMAT.

  66 data-name-1 <u>RENAMES</u> data-name-2 [<u>THRU</u> data-name-3]

COMMENTS.

The RENAMES clause is used to give an alternative name to one or more consecutive data fields.

When this clause is used data-name-2 (THRU to data-name-3) are given the name data-name-1. These areas of data may be referred to as the renamed version or as the original data names.

One or more RENAMES clause may be associated with any logical record, and must follow that record's last data description entry.

A level 66 RENAMES entry may not rename a level 01, level 77, level 88 or another level 66 entry.

The OCCURS clause may not be associated with the renamed items.

EXAMPLES.

```
    01 REC-A.
       03 FLD-1          PIC 99.
       03 FLD-2          PIC 9(3)V99.
       03 FLD-3          PIC X.
    66 NME-X RENAMES FLD-1 THRU FLD-2.
.
    01 REC-B.
       03 GRP-1.
          05 FLD-7       PIC 99.
          05 FLD-8       PIC XX.
       03 FLD-9          PIC X(7).
       03 FLD-10         PIC X(4).
    66 NME-Y RENAMES FLD-8 THRU FLD-10.
```

NOTES.

DATA DIVISION   **Level 88 condition-names**

FORMAT.

$$88 \text{ condition-name} \left\{ \begin{array}{l} \underline{\text{VALUE IS}} \\ \underline{\text{VALUES ARE}} \end{array} \right\} \text{lit-1} \left[\left\{ \begin{array}{l} \underline{\text{THROUGH}} \\ \underline{\text{THRU}} \end{array} \right\} \text{lit-2} \right]$$

$$\left[\text{lit-3} \left[\left\{ \begin{array}{l} \underline{\text{THROUGH}} \\ \underline{\text{THRU}} \end{array} \right\} \text{lit-4} \right] \right] \ldots$$

COMMENTS.

In the level 88 entry a condition-name is assigned to certain values held in a data item. This condition-name may be tested in the Procedure Division and the logic path of the program altered accordingly.

If at run-time the data item holds one of the values specified by the level 88 entry, then the condition is true, and if not, the condition is said to be false. The condition is tested in the Procedure Division by the IF, PERFORM and SEARCH verbs.

Inclusive ranges of values may be tested by using the THROUGH option. Different ranges may overlap if desired.

The data-items tested may be an elementary item, or under certain conditions a group item. These conditions are that the condition value must be a nonnumeric literal or figurative constant, the size of the condition value must not exceed the sum of the sizes of the elementary items within the group, and lastly, none of the items within the group have JUSTIFIED, SYNCHRONISED or USAGE, other than DISPLAY, clauses.

DATA DIVISION   Level 88 condition-names cont.

EXAMPLES.

```
DATA DIVISION.

    03 DESTINATION-CODE     PIC 99.
       88 HOME              VALUE 0 THRU 30.
       88 ABROAD            VALUE 40 THRU 50
                                  55
                                  60 THRU 70.

PROCEDURE DIVISION.

    IF HOME PERFORM PACK-ROUTINE-A.
    IF ABROAD PERFORM PACK-ROUTINE-B.
    ELSE PERFORM INV-DEST-ROUT.
```

NOTES.

PROCEDURE DIVISION

FORMAT.

<u>PROCEDURE</u> <u>DIVISION</u> [<u>USING</u> identifier-1
                             [identifier-2]...].

1. With sections.

[paragraph-name. [sentence]...]...

{section-name <u>SECTION</u> [segment-number].

[paragraph-name. [sentence]...]...}...

2. Without sections.

{paragraph-name. [sentence]...}...

3. With declaratives.

<u>DECLARATIVES</u>. {declarative-section}

<u>END</u> <u>DECLARATIVES</u>.

{section-name <u>SECTION</u> [segment-number].

[paragraph-name. [sentence]...]...}...

COMMENTS.

The execution of a program begins at the first executable statement following the Procedure Division header. The program run will continue until either a STOP statement or a run-time error is encountered. If the program has been called by another program the execution may be terminated by a EXIT PROGRAM statement.

The USING option allows the passing of parameters between a called program and a calling program. See CALL Page 104.

The Procedure Division can be organised in three possible ways.

1. It may consist of zero or more paragraphs followed by a number of sections. Each section being subdivided into one or more paragraphs.

PROCEDURE DIVISION cont.

COMMENTS cont.

2. It may consist only of paragraphs.

3. It may consist of a DECLARATIVES section and a series of sections.

DECLARATIVES section is defined on Page 98.
Sections, paragraphs, sentences and statements are defined as below:

SECTIONS   A section consists of section-header followed by one or more paragraphs. A section-header consists of a section-name, conforming to procedure-name formation rules, followed by the word SECTION and an optional segment-number. The segment-number (or priority-number) is a number in the range 0-49 and is used in segmented programs to indicate the most frequently used segments. The lower the segment number the more it is used. A segment limit can be defined in the OBJECT-COMPUTER paragraph and indicates a limit number below which all segments are permanently resident in main-storage. Each section-name must be unique.

PARAGRAPH   A paragraph consists of a paragraph-name followed by zero or more sentences. A paragraph-name is a user defined word and if sections are used it need not be unique since it can be qualified.

SENTENCE   A sentence consists of one or more statements terminated by a period and a space.

STATEMENT   A statement consists of a syntactically valid set of words (identifiers, figurative constants, etc.) and symbols (relational operators, etc.) beginning with a COBOL verb. Statements may be imperative (indicating unconditional action to be taken) or conditional.

PROCEDURE DIVISION cont.

EXAMPLES.

```
PROCEDURE DIVISION.

    PERFORM INITIALIZE.
    PERFORM PROCESS.

INITIALIZE SECTION.
INIT-PARA1.

INIT-PARA2.

PROCESS SECTION.
PROC-PARA1.

PROC-PARA2.
```

NOTES.

PROCEDURE DIVISION WITH DECLARATIVES (USE)

FORMAT.

PROCEDURE DIVISION [USING identifier-1
                           [identifier-2]...].
DECLARATIVES.

{section-name SECTION [segment-number]. USE sentence.

[paragraph-name. [sentence]...]...}...

END DECLARATIVES.

COMMENTS.

The DECLARATIVES section is used to provide procedures which are executed upon exceptional input/output conditions, with debugging procedures, and with the Report Writer.

All declarative procedures are preceded by the word DECLARATIVES, which must follow the Procedure Division header, and terminated by END DECLARATIVES.

The USE sentence defines the conditions that will cause execution of the immediately following paragraphs. The general format of the USE sentence for exception and error is:

$$\text{USE AFTER STANDARD} \begin{Bmatrix} \text{EXCEPTION} \\ \text{ERROR} \end{Bmatrix} \text{PROCEDURE ON} \begin{Bmatrix} \text{file-name-1...} \\ \text{INPUT} \\ \text{OUTPUT} \\ \text{I-O} \\ \text{EXTEND} \end{Bmatrix}$$

The general format of the USE sentence for the Report Writer is:

$$\text{USE FOR DEBUGGING ON} \begin{Bmatrix} \text{[ALL REFERENCES OF] identifier-1} \\ \text{file-name-1} \\ \text{procedure-name-1} \\ \text{ALL PROCEDURES} \\ \text{cd-name-1} \end{Bmatrix} ...$$

The general format of the USE sentence for the Report Writer is:

USE BEFORE REPORTING identifier

PROCEDURE DIVISION WITH DECLARATIVES (USE) cont.

COMMENTS cont.

(NOTE: cd-name-1 is a message control system interface area described within the Communication Section).

EXAMPLE.

   .
   .
PROCEDURE DIVISION.
DECLARATIVES.
CHECKING SECTION. USE FOR DEBUGGING ON ALL
                                                  PROCEDURES.
PARA1.
   .
   .
   .
PARA2.
   .
   .
END DECLARATIVES.

NOTES.

PROCEDURE DIVISION   **ACCEPT**

FORMAT.

```
                               ⎧ mnemonic-name ⎫
                               ⎪ DATE          ⎪
    ACCEPT identifier [FROM    ⎨ DAY           ⎬ ]
                               ⎩ TIME          ⎭
```

COMMENTS.

The ACCEPT verb allows execution time acquisition of data in an interactive manner. The data accepted is placed in the identifier which must be defined in the data division. The rules for data acceptance are the same as in the MOVE statement, with the exception that if the transferred data has a size less than the receiving field, then additional data is requested.

If the FROM option is omitted then at execution time the program will halt until response is given.

If the FROM mnemonic-name option is used then an explicit device name is stated, such as the CONSOLE. The device name must be referenced in the SPECIAL-NAMES paragraph.

When the DATE, DAY or TIME options are used then the current day, date or time is placed in the identifier. The date is in the form YYMMDD, day is in the form YYDDD (where YY is the last two digits of the year and DDD is the number of days in the year), and time is given in the form HHMMSSFF (where FF is hundredths of a second).

The ACCEPT verb is often used with the DISPLAY verb.

EXAMPLES.

- DISPLAY "PLEASE ENTER YOUR SURNAME".
  ACCEPT S-NAME.
- ACCEPT IN-DATE FROM DATE.

NOTES.

PROCEDURE DIVISION   **ADD**

FORMAT.

1. <u>ADD</u> {identifier-1 / literal-1} [identifier-2 / literal-2] ...

                     <u>TO</u> {identifier-m [<u>ROUNDED</u>]} ...

                     [ON <u>SIZE</u> <u>ERROR</u> imperative-statement]

2. <u>ADD</u> {identifier-1 / literal-1} {identifier-2 / literal-2} [identifier-3 / literal-3] ...

                     <u>GIVING</u> {identifier-m [<u>ROUNDED</u>]} ...

                     [ON <u>SIZE</u> <u>ERROR</u> imperative-statement]

3. <u>ADD</u> {<u>CORRESPONDING</u> / <u>CORR</u>} identifier-1 <u>TO</u>

                     <u>TO</u> identifier-2 [<u>ROUNDED</u>]

                     [ON <u>SIZE</u> <u>ERROR</u> imperative-statement]

COMMENTS.

Format-1 will add the sum of identifier-1 identifier-2 etc., to identifier-m, identifier-n, etc.

Format-2 will add identifier-1, identifier-2 etc., and place the sum in identifier-m, identifier-n, etc.

Format-3 will add all corresponding items of group identifier-1 to corresponding items of group identifier-2. The rules noted in the CORRESPONDING option (Page 112) have to be adhered to.

The ROUNDED option rounds the result to the nearest character as described in the receiving fields PICTURE.

The ON SIZE ERROR option allows an imperative statement, or set of statements, to be executed should the result overflow the receiving field.

If the ROUNDED option is specified, then the rounding is carried out before any size error is checked.

All identifiers used should be elementary numeric items, except when the GIVING clause is stated in which

PROCEDURE DIVISION   **ADD cont.**

COMMENTS cont.

case the receiving field may be an edited numeric item.
Decimal point alignment is carried out automatically.

EXAMPLES.

    .
    .
    ADD A,B TO C ROUNDED.
    .
    ADD M,N,O,P GIVING Q ON SIZE ERROR GO TO STOP-PROG.
    .
    ADD A TO B ROUNDED ON SIZE ERROR GO TO PARA-1.
    .
    ADD A,B TO C ROUNDED D.
    .
    ADD CORRESPONDING GRP-1 TO GRP-2.
    .
    .

NOTES.

PROCEDURE DIVISION   **ALTER**

FORMAT.

ALTER procedure-name-1 TO [PROCEED TO] procedure-name-2

[procedure-name-3 TO [PROCEED TO] procedure-name-4]...

COMMENTS.

The ALTER statement modifies a predetermined sequence of operations.

Procedure-name-1, procedure-name-3, etc. are single sentence paragraphs consisting only of a GO TO statement, without the DEPENDING phrase.

Procedure-name-2, procedure-name-4, etc. are the names of sections or paragraphs in the Procedure Division.

After the execution of an ALTER statement the destination of the GO TO statement is altered to procedure-name-2 etc.

The ALTER statement is generally recognised as being dangerous as it alters predetermined logic paths and makes logic difficult to follow.

EXAMPLE.

```
      .
      PARA-1.
          GO TO PARA-2
      .
      .
      .
      PARA-2
      .
          ALTER PARA-1 TO PROCEED TO PARA-3.
      .
```

NOTES.

PROCEDURE DIVISION   **CALL**

FORMAT.

$$\underline{\text{CALL}} \begin{Bmatrix} \text{identifier-1} \\ \text{literal-1} \end{Bmatrix} [\underline{\text{USING}}\ \text{data-name-1}\ [\text{data-name-2}]...]$$

$$[\text{ON}\ \underline{\text{OVERFLOW}}\ \text{imperative-statement}]$$

COMMENTS.

The CALL statement causes control to be transferred from a calling program to a called sub-program in the object program library.

Identifier-1 or literal-1 specifies the name of the called sub-program.

The USING option specifies passed parameters between the two programs.

The ON OVERFLOW imperative-statement is executed should the available object time memory be unable to accomodate the called sub-program.

The called sub-program may be written in any language, but if it is in COBOL it will differ from a normal COBOL program in two ways:

1. The external variables (i.e. the passed parameters) must be level 01 or elementary data items, defined in the LINKAGE SECTION and must also be referenced in the Procedure Division header with the following format:

<u>PROCEDURE</u> <u>DIVISION</u> [<u>USING</u> parameter-1 [parameter-2]...]

2. Control is returned to the calling program upon execution of the <u>EXIT</u> <u>PROGRAM</u> statement.

The passed parameters must be defined in both the calling program and the called program. The order of appearance of the passed parameters in the USING phrase of the CALL statement and the USING phrase of the Procedure Division header is important as the correspondence is positional and not by name. The PICTURE's of the parameters in the calling and called program do not have to be identical although they must correspond in terms of the data being moved. Index names may be used as parameters. The state of the parameters within a called program remains unaltered until that program is again called, or the CANCEL statement is used.

PROCEDURE DIVISION   **CALL cont.**

COMMENTS cont.

The CALL verb is also used with modular programming techniques when separate modules are compiled separately.

EXAMPLE.
  .
        CALL "SUB-PROG" USING FIELD-1.

below is the relevant section from the called sub-program.
  .
    WORKING-STORAGE SECTION.
  .
    LINKAGE SECTION.
    01   PARAM1   PIC XX.
  .
    PROCEDURE DIVISION USING PARAM1.
  .
  .
        EXIT PROGRAM.
  .

NOTES

PROCEDURE DIVISION   **CANCEL**

FORMAT.

$$\underline{\text{CANCEL}} \begin{Bmatrix} \text{identifier-1} \\ \text{literal-1} \end{Bmatrix} \begin{bmatrix} \text{identifier-2} \\ \text{literal-2} \end{bmatrix} \ldots$$

COMMENTS.

The CANCEL statement allows the release of storage areas occupied by called sub-programs.

Identifier-1, (or literal-1) etc. defines the name of the program whose area is to be released.

The sub-program may again be called using the CALL statement. In this case the called program is set to an initialised state.

EXAMPLES.

.

CANCEL "INIT-PROG".

.

CANCEL NAMEPRG1, NAMEPRG2.

.

NOTES.

PROCEDURE DIVISION   **CLOSE**

FORMAT.

$$\text{CLOSE file-name-1} \left[\begin{Bmatrix} \underline{\text{REEL}} \\ \underline{\text{UNIT}} \end{Bmatrix} \begin{bmatrix} \text{WITH NO } \underline{\text{REWIND}} \\ \text{FOR } \underline{\text{REMOVAL}} \end{bmatrix} \atop \text{WITH} \quad \begin{Bmatrix} \text{NO } \underline{\text{REWIND}} \\ \underline{\text{LOCK}} \end{Bmatrix} \right] \ldots$$

COMMENTS.

The CLOSE statement causes the closure and release of files from a program.

On closure of an output file the CLOSE statement usually causes trailer records to be written at the end of the file. Strictly, however, this is implementor defined.

Magnetic tape files are rewound unless with WITH NO REWIND option is included. The options REEL or UNIT are specified only for physical sequential multivolume files. The terms REEL and UNIT are interchangeable. The FOR REMOVAL option is used to indicate to the operator that the tape file can be removed.

If the WITH LOCK option is used the file cannot be re-opened for the duration of the current job.

If an attempt is made to CLOSE a file which has not yet been opened an execution error will occur.

EXAMPLES.

    .
    CLOSE FILE-A, FILE-B.
    CLOSE MAG-FILE WITH NO REWIND.
    CLOSE ONCE-FILE WITH LOCK.
    .

NOTES.

PROCEDURE DIVISION   **COMPUTE**

FORMAT.

COMPUTE identifier-1[ROUNDED][identifier-2[ROUNDED]]...

$$= \begin{Bmatrix} \text{identifier-m} \\ \text{literal} \\ \text{arithmetic-expression} \end{Bmatrix}$$

[ON SIZE ERROR imperative-statement]

COMMENTS.

The COMPUTE statement places identifier-m, a literal, or the result of an arithmetic expression in identifier-1, identifier-2, etc.

An arithmetic expression is a string of identifiers or literals connected by arithmetic operators. All arithmetic operators must have a space on either side. Valid arithmetic operators are:

```
        +   addition
        -   subtraction
        /   division
        *   multiplication
        **  exponentiation

        +   unary plus (multiplication by +1)
        -   unary minus (multiplication by -1)
```

Evaluation of an arithmetic expression (which may contain parenthesis) takes place from left to right within the following hierarchy:

```
        1. Parenthesis
        2. Unary plus and minus
        3. **
        4. * and /
        5. + and -
```

The ROUNDED option rounds the result to the nearest character as described in the receiving field's PICTURE.

The ON SIZE ERROR option indicates the execution of any imperative-statement should the result overflow the receiving field.

PROCEDURE DIVISION   **COMPUTE** cont.

COMMENTS cont.

If more than one identifier is specified for the
resultant fields, then the value of the arithmetic
expression is computed and the value stored, in turn,
in identifier-1, identifier-2, etc.

EXAMPLE.

- COMPUTE FIELD-1 = A ** 2 / (B + D + C).
- COMPUTE ANSW ROUNDED = FIELD-A.
- COMPUTE A = B * C ON SIZE ERROR DISPLAY "SIZE ERROR-A".
- COMPUTE A ROUNDED, B = C * D * E.

NOTES.

PROCEDURE DIVISION   COPY

FORMAT.

COPY text-name $\left\{ \begin{array}{c} \underline{OF} \\ \underline{IN} \end{array} \right\}$ [library-name]

[REPLACING $\left\{\left[\begin{array}{l} \text{<<pseudo-text-1>>} \\ \text{identifier-1} \\ \text{literal-1} \\ \text{word-1} \end{array}\right] \underline{BY} \left\{\begin{array}{l} \text{<<pseudo-text-2>>} \\ \text{identifier-2} \\ \text{literal-2} \\ \text{word-2} \end{array}\right\}\right\}...$]

COMMENTS.

The COPY verb allows the insertion of pre-coded COBOL statements into a program. These pre-coded statements are held on a library file. Thus sections of coding which are frequently used (e.g. certain record layouts or special calculations) need only be coded once, entered into the library, and thereafter can be copied into any program. The COPY statement may appear anywhere in the source program.

The copied coding must be syntactically correct and must be logically consistent with the recipient program.

The text-name must follow the rules for formation of a file-name and if more than one library is available to the program during compilation then the text-name must be qualified by the library-name.

COPY statements may not be nested. That is, coding which is copied into a program using a COPY verb may not itself contain a COPY statement.

Using the REPLACING option pseudo-text, literals, identifiers or COBOL words from the copied text may be replaced.

Pseudo-text-1 may be any string of text from the library entry bounded by pseudo-text delimiters (<< and >> or == and ==).

The identifiers referred to in the REPLACING option may be defined in any Data Division section. Each literal may be numeric or non-numeric. Each word may be any single COBOL word.

PROCEDURE DIVISION   COPY cont.

EXAMPLES.

If the coding below is entered on the library (UTIL)
under the name ENTRY1
```
    01   LAYOUT-A.
         02 ITEM-1              PIC X(9).
         02 ITEM-2              PIC 9(8).
         02 ITEM-3              PIC 9V99.
```

and the coding below is also entered in the library
(UTIL) under the name ENTRY2
```
    PARA-READ.
         READ INPUT-FILE AT END DISPLAY "FINISH"
                              GO TO END-PARA.
```

Below are examples of how these entries may be used in
a source program.
```
    .
    .
    FD INPUT-FILE
    COPY ENTRY1 OF UTIL REPLACING ITEM-1 BY ITEM-1B
    .
    .
    PROCEDURE DIVISION.
    .
    .
    COPY ENTRY2 OF UTIL REPLACING
                    <<PARA-READ>> BY <<PARA-1>>
                    <<FINISH>>    BY <<END>>.
```

These entries would yield
```
    .
    .
    FD INPUT-FILE.
    01 LAYOUT-A.
       02 ITEM-1B             PIC X(9).
       02 ITEM-2              PIC 9(8).
       02 ITEM-3              PIC 9V99.
    .
    .
    PROCEDURE DIVISION.
    .
    .
    PARA-1.
         READ INPUT-FILE AT END DISPLAY "END"
                              GO TO END-PARA.
    .
```

NOTES.

PROCEDURE DIVISION   **CORRESPONDING OPTION**

FORMAT.

$$\text{ADD} \begin{Bmatrix} \underline{\text{CORRESPONDING}} \\ \underline{\text{CORR}} \end{Bmatrix} \text{identifier-1}$$
                                           <u>TO</u> identifier-2 [<u>ROUNDED</u>]
                                           [<u>ON SIZE ERROR</u> imperative-statement]

$$\text{SUBTRACT} \begin{Bmatrix} \underline{\text{CORRESPONDING}} \\ \underline{\text{CORR}} \end{Bmatrix} \text{identifier-1}$$
                                           <u>FROM</u> identifier-2 [<u>ROUNDED</u>]
                                           [<u>ON SIZE ERROR</u> imperative-statement]

$$\underline{\text{MOVE}} \begin{Bmatrix} \underline{\text{CORRESPONDING}} \\ \underline{\text{CORR}} \end{Bmatrix} \text{identifier-1} \underline{\text{TO}} \text{ identifier-2}$$

COMMENTS.

The CORRESPONDING option can be used with the verbs ADD, SUBTRACT, or MOVE.

This option allows all corresponding elementary data-items in group identifier-1 to be added, subtracted or moved with all corresponding elementary data-items within group identifier-2.

For two items to be corresponding the following conditions must apply:
    a) The items should have the same name and level.
    b) In the case of ADD or SUBTRACT they must both be elementary.
    c) In the case of MOVE at least one must be elementary.
    d) The items do not include REDEFINES, RENAMES, OCCURS or USAGE IS INDEX clauses.

PROCEDURE DIVISION   **CORRESPONDING OPTION cont.**

EXAMPLES.

```
    .
    .
    01  GRP1.
        03 ITEM-A              PIC 999.
        03 ITEM-B              PIC 99.
    .
    .
    01  GRP2.
        03 ITEM-A              PIC 999.
        03 FILLER              PIC XX.
        03 ITEM-B              PIC 99.
        .
        .
        MOVE CORRESPONDING GRP1 TO GRP2.
```

NOTES.

PROCEDURE DIVISION   **DELETE**

FORMAT.

    <u>DELETE</u> file-name RECORD
                        [<u>INVALID</u> KEY imperative-statement]

COMMENTS.

The DELETE statement is used to remove a record from an indexed or relative file.

<u>Indexed Files</u>.

For an indexed file under sequential access the most recently read record will be deleted upon execution of a DELETE statement. The INVALID KEY clause does not apply in such cases.

For dynamic or random access of an indexed file the DELETE statement will remove the record with the specified RECORD KEY. If no key match is found the INVALID KEY clause is invoked.

<u>Relative Files</u>.

For a relative file under sequential access the most recently read record will be deleted upon execution of the DELETE statement. The INVALID KEY clause does not apply in such cases.

For dynamic or random access of an indexed file the DELETE statement will remove the record with the specified RELATIVE KEY. If no key match is found the INVALID KEY clause is invoked.

For both indexed and relative files the DELETE verb causes the FILE STATUS data item to be updated.

EXAMPLES.
                       Sequential access

```
   READ FILE-A AT END GO TO EOF.
   IF FIELD-A = "X" DELETE FILE-A RECORD.
```
                   Dynamic or random access

```
   MOVE KEY-VALUE TO RECORD-KEY AREA.
   DELETE FILE-B RECORD INVALID KEY PERFORM ERR-R.
```

NOTES.

PROCEDURE DIVISION   **DISPLAY**

FORMAT.

$$\underline{\text{DISPLAY}} \left\{ \begin{array}{l} \text{identifier-1} \\ \text{literal-1} \end{array} \right\} \left[\begin{array}{l} \text{identifier-2} \\ \text{literal-2} \end{array} \right] \ldots$$

$$[\underline{\text{UPON}} \text{ mnemonic-name}]$$

COMMENTS.

The DISPLAY verb is used to output low volumes of data at execution-time. The output is directed to a logical system output device (normally the operators console) unless the UPON option is used in which case the output is sent to the mnemonic-name device, which is defined in the SPECIAL-NAMES paragraph.

The DISPLAY verb is often used with the ACCEPT verb to produce execution-time interactive communication.

EXAMPLES.

   .
   .
   DISPLAY "THE DATE IS" MACHINE-DATE.
   .
   DISPLAY "WHAT IS YOUR NAME".
   ACCEPT NAME-IN.
   DISPLAY "THANK YOU".
   .
   .

NOTES.

PROCEDURE DIVISION   **DIVIDE**

FORMAT.

1. <u>DIVIDE</u> {identifier-1 / literal-1} <u>INTO</u> identifier-2 [<u>ROUNDED</u>]

    [identifier-3 [<u>ROUNDED</u>]]

    [ON <u>SIZE</u> <u>ERROR</u> imperative-statement]

2. <u>DIVIDE</u> {identifier-1 / literal-1} {<u>BY</u> / <u>INTO</u>} {identifier-2 / literal-2}

    <u>GIVING</u> identifier-3 [<u>ROUNDED</u>]

    [identifier-4 [<u>ROUNDED</u>]]...

    [ON <u>SIZE</u> <u>ERROR</u> imperative-statement]

3. <u>DIVIDE</u> {identifier-1 / literal-1} {<u>BY</u> / <u>INTO</u>} {identifier-2 / literal-2}

    <u>GIVING</u> identifier-3 [<u>ROUNDED</u>]

    <u>REMAINDER</u> identifier-4

    [ON <u>SIZE</u> <u>ERROR</u> imperative-statement]

COMMENTS.

The DIVIDE verb is used to divide one numeric data item into another and sets the values of data items equal to the quotient and remainder.

Each literal must be numeric and each identifier must be an elementary numeric except those associated with the GIVING and REMAINDER phrases which may be elementary numeric or elementary numeric edited items.

In Format-1 identifier-1 or literal-1 is divided, in turn, into identifier-2, identifier-3 etc., and the result placed in identifier-2, identifier-3 etc.

In Format-2 identifier-1 or literal-1 is divided by or into identifier-2 or literal-2 and the quotient placed in identifier-3 and identifier-4 etc., if specified.

In Format-3 identifier-1 or literal-1 is divided by or into identifier-2 or literal-2 and the quotient placed in identifier-3. The remainder, here defined as the

PROCEDURE DIVISION   **DIVIDE cont.**

COMMENTS cont.

result of subtracting the product of the quotient and the divisor from the dividend, is placed in identifier-4.

The ROUNDED phrase allows the rounding of the last digit of the resultant field. When REMAINDER is used with rounding the quotient used in the remainder calculation is truncated rather than rounded.

The ON SIZE ERROR causes the execution of any imperative statement should the result of the division, after any specified rounding, exceed the size of the resultant field. Division by zero will cause an on size error.

EXAMPLES.

```
.
DIVIDE 20 INTO FIELD-1 FIELD-2 FIELD-3.
.
DIVIDE ITEM-A BY ITEM-B GIVING ITEM-C ROUNDED
          ON SIZE ERROR PERFORM FAULT-ROUTINE.
.
DIVIDE NUMB-1 BY 27 GIVING RES-FIELD
          REMAINDER REM-FIELD.
```

NOTES.

PROCEDURE DIVISION ENTER

FORMAT.

    <u>ENTER</u> language-name [routine-name].

COMMENTS.

The ENTER verb is used to allow a new programming language to be used within a program. It can also be used to call a subroutine into a program, which is written in a different language.

When the secondary language is inserted at coding time then the secondary language statements are coded following the ENTER verb.

Control is returned to COBOL when an ENTER COBOL statement is encountered.

When a subroutine is called the secondary code is incorporated, in-line into the object program. The secondary code is, in this case, also in object form.

EXAMPLE.

```
       .
       .
       .
    ENTER FORTRAN.
    IF (INUM-100)7,7,9       FORTRAN statement
 9  IFLD=INUM-10             FORTRAN statement
       .
       .
    ENTER COBOL
       .
       .
    ENTER ASSEMBLER BINCALS-ROUT.
       .
       .
       .
```

NOTES.

PROCEDURE DIVISION   **EXIT**

FORMAT.

> EXIT [PROGRAM]

COMMENTS.

The EXIT statement is used as an end point for a procedure or set of procedures. It is mainly used to signify the return point for a set of PERFORMed procedures.

If the PROGRAM option is used then the program being executed has been called by another program and upon execution of the statement control will be returned to the calling program.

The EXIT statement must be the only statement in a paragraph.

EXAMPLES.

```
        .
        PERFORM PARA-1 THROUGH PARA-1-END.
        .
        .
    PARA-1.
        .
    PARA-1-END.
        EXIT.
    PARA-2.
        .
        .
    PARA-2-END.
        EXIT PROGRAM.
```

NOTES.

PROCEDURE DIV.   GENERATE, INITIATE, SUPPRESS, TERMINATE

FORMAT.

<u>GENERATE</u>   {data-name / report-name}

<u>INITIATE</u>   report-name-1 [report-name-2]...

<u>SUPPRESS</u>   PRINTING

<u>TERMINATE</u> report-name-1 [report-name-2]...

COMMENTS.

These four verbs are used specifically to deal with the Report Writer capabilities of COBOL in the Procedure Division.

Reports generated in a COBOL program must be set up with the appropriate File Section FD and Report Section RD entries. These are described fully starting on Page 38 and 54.

INITIATE initialises the page counter and instructs the printing of the headings on the first page.

The GENERATE statement causes a report to be produced in the format specified in the Report Section. If the data-name is given then detail-reporting is performed and if the report-name is specified, summary-reporting is performed.

In detail-reporting the detail line is printed upon encountering the GENERATE statement and all other lines (at control breaks etc.) are printed automatically.

In summary-reporting the detail lines are not printed but control break lines and appropriate headings are printed.

The TERMINATE statement completes the processing of a report and acts as a control break for all control fields.

The SUPPRESS statement inhibits the printing of a report group.

PROCEDURE DIV.   GENERATE, INITIATE, SUPPRESS, TERMINATE

EXAMPLE.
```
    .
    .
    FILE SECTION.
    FD  IN-FILE
    .
    .
    FD  REPORT-FILE   LABEL RECORDS OMITTED
                      REPORT IS COMPANY REPORT.
    .
    .
    REPORT SECTION.
    RD  COMPANY-REPORT, CONTROLS ARE FINAL, DEPT,
                        PAGE LIMIT IS 50 LINES.
    01  TYPE PAGE HEADING.
        03 LINE-1
         .
         .
    01  TYPE CONTROL FOOTING DEPT LINE PLUS 1.
        03 COLUMN-12
         .
         .
    PROCEDURE DIVISION.
        .
        .
        OPEN INPUT IN-FILE, OUTPUT REPORT-FILE.
        INITIATE COMPANY REPORT.
    READ-FILE.
        READ IN-FILE AT END GO TO CLOSE-DOWN.
        GENERATE COMPANY-REPORT.
        GO TO READ-FILE.
    .
    .
```

NOTES.

PROCEDURE DIVISION   **GO TO (DEPENDING ON)**

FORMAT.

1. <u>GO</u> TO procedure-name

2. <u>GO</u> TO procedure-name-1 [procedure-name-2]...

<u>DEPENDING</u> ON identifier

COMMENTS.

The GO TO statement is used to transfer control to a paragraph or section. When the GO TO is executed the control will continue at the first executable statement of the specified paragraph or section.

The identifier must be an elementary numeric integer.

With format 2 the transfer of control is to the procedure-name corresponding to the numeric value of the identifier. If the identifier has a value of 1 control is passed to procedure-name-1, if the identifier has a value of 2 control is passed to procedure-name-2, and so on. If the identifier has a higher numeric value than the number of procedure names specified, or has a value less than 1, then control passes to the next statement after the GO TO statement.

EXAMPLE.

```
     GO TO PARA-1.
        .
PARA-1.
        .
     GO TO PARA-A, PARA-B, PARA-C, DEPENDING ON FLD-X
        .
PARA-A.
        .
PARA-B.
        .
PARA-C.
        .
```

NOTES.

PROCEDURE DIVISION   **IF**

FORMAT.

IF condition $\begin{Bmatrix} \text{statement-1 ...} \\ \underline{\text{NEXT SENTENCE}} \end{Bmatrix}$ [$\underline{\text{ELSE}}$ $\begin{Bmatrix} \text{statement-2 ...} \\ \underline{\text{NEXT SENTENCE}} \end{Bmatrix}$]

COMMENTS.

The IF verb evaluates a condition and if that condition is true then control is passed to statement-1 (or the first NEXT SENTENCE option). The ELSE option can only be invoked when the condition is false.

Statement-1 and statement-2 may be a list of statements.

The ELSE option may be omitted and the IF statement terminated by a full stop after the first braces, if required.

Whenever NEXT SENTENCE is encountered control is passed to the beginning of the sentence immediately following that one containing the IF sentence.

The IF statement must be terminated by a full stop unless it is itself part of another IF statement.

Testable conditions are discussed in more detail on Page 13.

IF statements may be nested. That is, IF statements may appear within other IF statements. Within nested combinations it is advisable that IF statements should be considered as paired IF and ELSE combinations indented across the page from left to right. Therefore an ELSE statement must be matched with the immediately preceding IF statement that has not already been paired with an ELSE. See examples.

The logic involved in nested IF statements is often very difficult to follow and complicated nestings should be avoided, and possibly replaced by a set of separate statements.

PROCEDURE DIVISION   **IF cont.**

EXAMPLES.

```
IF FIELD-A = FIELD-B GO TO PARA-P.

IF ITEM-A > 100 GO TO PROCESS-PARA
ELSE ADD 1 TO ITEM-1.


IF COUNT-1 = 0 OR COUNT-2 = 0 GO TO END-IT.


IF L = 1

   IF J = 2 GO TO PARA-1
   ELSE     GO TO PARA-2

ELSE

   IF K = 4 GO TO PARA-4
   ELSE     GO TO PARA-5.


IF A > B ADD F TO G           - Unmatched so if false
                                next sentence is
                                executed
   IF A = B

      IF B = C ADD B TO C
      ELSE    ADD B TO D

   ELSE

      IF B = D ADD C TO E     - Unmatched so if false
                                next sentence is
                                executed
         IF D = E ADD D TO E
         ELSE    ADD E TO F.
```

NOTES.

PROCEDURE DIVISION   **INSPECT**

FORMAT.

INSPECT identifier-1

   [TALLYING {identifier-2

              FOR $\left\{ \begin{Bmatrix} \underline{ALL} \\ \underline{LEADING} \\ \underline{CHARACTERS} \end{Bmatrix} \begin{Bmatrix} identifier\text{-}3 \\ literal\text{-}1 \end{Bmatrix} \right\}$

                 [$\begin{Bmatrix} \underline{BEFORE} \\ \underline{AFTER} \end{Bmatrix}$ INITIAL $\begin{Bmatrix} ident\text{-}4 \\ lit\text{-}2 \end{Bmatrix}$]}...}...]

   [REPLACING

$\left\{ \begin{matrix} \underline{CHARACTERS}\ \underline{BY} \begin{Bmatrix} identifier\text{-}6 \\ literal\text{-}4 \end{Bmatrix} \\ \qquad [\begin{Bmatrix} \underline{BEFORE} \\ \underline{AFTER} \end{Bmatrix} \text{INITIAL} \begin{Bmatrix} ident\text{-}7 \\ lit\text{-}5 \end{Bmatrix}] \\ \begin{Bmatrix} \underline{ALL} \\ \underline{LEADING} \\ \underline{FIRST} \end{Bmatrix} \begin{Bmatrix} identifier\text{-}5 \\ literal\text{-}3 \end{Bmatrix} \underline{BY} \begin{Bmatrix} ident\text{-}6 \\ lit\text{-}4 \end{Bmatrix} \\ \qquad [\begin{Bmatrix} \underline{BEFORE} \\ \underline{AFTER} \end{Bmatrix} \text{INITIAL} \begin{Bmatrix} ident\text{-}7 \\ lit\text{-}5 \end{Bmatrix}]\}... \end{matrix} \right\}$...]

COMMENTS.

The INSPECT statement provides the facility to tally (count), replace, or tally and replace occurrences of characters within a data item.

Identifier-1 is the inspected item and either the TALLYING or REPLACING option, or both, must be specified. When both are specified the tallying is carried out before the replacing.

Identifier-1 must be an elementary or group item with DISPLAY usage.

PROCEDURE DIVISION INSPECT cont.

COMMENTS cont.

TALLYING option.

The TALLYING option will inspect identifier-1 and increment the number of occurrences of certain characters to the elementary integer count-field indentifier-2. Identifier-2 is not initialised by this statement. Identifier-3 or literal-1 is the tallying field and if a figurative constant is used it is assumed to be a one-character nonnumeric literal.

If ALL is specified then for all occurrences of the tallying field within the inspected item the count field will be increased by 1.
If LEADING is specified then tallying is carried out from left to right until a mismatch is found.
If CHARACTERS is specified then the count field is incremented by 1 for each character in the inspected item.
If the BEFORE option is specified tallying proceeds left to right until the occurrence of the delimiting identifier or literal. If the AFTER option is specified tallying does not begin until the delimiting identifier or literal is encountered on a left to right inspection.

REPLACING option.

The REPLACING option will replace certain occurrences of characters within identifier-1 by other specified characters.
If CHARACTERS is specified then all characters within the inspected item will be replaced by those specified by identifier-6 or literal-4.
If ALL is specified then all occurrences of identifier-5 or literal-3 within the inspected field will be replaced by those specified by identifier-6 or literal-4.
If LEADING is specified then replacement will occur left to right until a mismatch is encountered.
If FIRST is specified only the first occurrence of the specified character is replaced.
With the BEFORE option replacement proceeds left to right until the delimiting identifier or literal is encountered.
With the AFTER option replacement only proceeds after the occurrence of the delimiter.

PROCEDURE DIVISION   **INSPECT cont.**

COMMENTS cont.

With both the TALLYING and REPLACING options when the BEFORE option is specified and yet the delimiter is not found then counting and/or replacing continues to the rightmost character. In the case of the AFTER option, if the delimiter is not found then no counting and/or replacement takes place.

EXAMPLES.

```
    .
    INSPECT RECORD-1
            TALLYING TALLY-FIELD
                FOR ALL SPACES.
    .
    INSPECT STOCK-NUMBER
            REPLACING LEADING SPACES BY ZEROES.
    .
    INSPECT RECORD-AREA
            TALLYING COUNT-AREA
                FOR ALL SPACES
                AFTER INITIAL "*"
            REPLACING ALL SPACES BY ZEROES
                AFTER INITIAL "*".
```

NOTES.

PROCEDURE DIVISION   **MERGE**

FORMAT.

$$\underline{\text{MERGE}}\ \text{file-name-1 ON} \begin{Bmatrix} \underline{\text{ASCENDING}} \\ \underline{\text{DESCENDING}} \end{Bmatrix} \text{KEY data-name-1} \\ [\text{data-name-2}]\ldots$$

$$[\text{ON} \begin{Bmatrix} \underline{\text{ASCENDING}} \\ \underline{\text{DESCENDING}} \end{Bmatrix} \text{KEY data-name-3} \\ [\text{data-name-4}]\ldots]\ldots$$

[COLLATING <u>SEQUENCE</u> IS alphabet-name]

<u>USING</u> file-name-2 file-name-3 [file-name-4]...

$$\begin{Bmatrix} \text{OUTPUT}\ \underline{\text{PROCEDURE}}\ \text{IS section-name-1} \\ \qquad\qquad\qquad\qquad\ \left[\begin{Bmatrix} \underline{\text{THROUGH}} \\ \underline{\text{THRU}} \end{Bmatrix}\ \text{section-name-2} \right] \\ \underline{\text{GIVING}}\quad \text{file-name-5} \end{Bmatrix}$$

COMMENTS.

The MERGE statement combines two or more identically sequenced files on one or more specified keys and makes records available in merged order to an output procedure or output file.

File-name-1 must be described with an SD (sort-merge file description) in the File Section of the program. File-name-2, file-name-3, etc., must be described in the File Section with FD entries and must already have been sorted according to an identical set of ascending or descending keys. The size of the records described for file-name-2, file-name-3, etc., and file-name-5 must be identical to that defined for file-name-1.

The result of the merge statement is that the records contained on file-name-2, file-name-3 etc., will be merged according to the specified key after being transferred to file-name-1. If the GIVING option is used the resultant merged file will be transferred to file-name-5 which has been described in the File Section with an ordinary FD entry.

If the OUTPUT PROCEDURE is used then it specifies the section-name(s) of a procedure which selects, modifies or copies the records which are output from the merge

PROCEDURE DIVISION   **MERGE cont.**

COMMENTS cont.

process. The output procedures deal with the merged records one at a time and a request for the next record is carried out with a RETURN statement. The output procedures may not contain any SORT or MERGE statements and may not be accessed by the program except by the MERGE (or SORT) statement.

The COLLATING SEQUENCE option specifies the collating sequence to be used in the nonnumeric comparisons of the key values. The alphabet-name must be specified in the SPECIAL-NAMES paragraph.

The files used in the merge operation should not be opened for the merge. The files are automatically opened and closed.

EXAMPLE.

```
      .
   MERGE WORK-FILE
         ASCENDING KEY DEPT
         ASCENDING KEY EMP-NO
         USING EMP-FILE-1 EMP-FILE-2
         GIVING EMPLOYEE MASTER.
      .
```

NOTES.

PROCEDURE DIVISION   MOVE

FORMAT.

1. <u>MOVE</u> {identifier-1 / literal} <u>TO</u> identifier-2 [identifier-3]...

2. <u>MOVE</u> {<u>CORRESPONDING</u> / <u>CORR</u>} identifier-1 <u>TO</u> identifier-2

COMMENTS.

The MOVE statement is used to move data from one area of main storage to another, and to perform conversions and/or editing on that data.

Identifier-1 and literal are the sending fields and identifier-2, identifier-3 etc., are the receiving fields.

When format-1 is used the identifiers may be elementary or group items. Format-2 allows the movement of one group of similarly named items to another group of similarly named items. See the CORRESPONDING option on Page 112.

When using Format-1 with more than one receiving field the data is moved firstly to identifier-2, then identifier-3 etc.

An index data-item cannot appear as the operand of a MOVE statement.

Indexed or subscripted data-items may appear in MOVE statements. The indexing or subscripting associated with a sending field is evaluated immediately before the move as is any indexing or subscripting associated with the receiving field.

Elementary Moves.

Any MOVE in which the sending and receiving items are both elementary items is an elementary move. Each elementary item belongs to one of the following categories: numeric, alphabetic, alphanumeric, numeric edited and alphanumeric edited.

A table of valid and invalid elementary moves is shown on the following page.

PROCEDURE DIVISION   **MOVE cont.**

COMMENTS cont.

Sending Item	Receiving Item					
	AB	AN	AE	NI	NN	NE
Alphabetic (AB)	YES	YES	YES	NO	NO	NO
Alphanumeric (AN)	YES	YES	YES	YES	YES	YES
Alphanumeric (AE) Edited	YES	YES	YES	NO	NO	NO
Numeric Integer (NI)	NO	YES	YES	YES	YES	YES
Numeric Noninteger (NN)	NO	NO	NO	YES	YES	YES
Numeric (NE) Edited	NO	YES	YES	NO	NO	NO

Valid and Invalid Elementary Moves.

As well as the above table there are other rules governing certain elementary rules.

For alphanumeric and alphanumeric edited receiving items:

- the data is aligned on the leftmost character position with rightmost space fill or truncation if the sending item is too long or too short respectively.

- if the sending item has an operational sign (whether SEPARATE CHARACTER or not) that sign will not be moved.

For numeric and numeric edited receiving items.

- the data is aligned on the decimal point with leftmost zero fill or editing if the sending field is smaller and with leftmost truncation if the sending field is longer.

- when the receiving item is a signed numeric the sign of the sending item is placed in the receiving item. If the sending item has no sign then a positive sign is generated.

PROCEDURE DIVISION   **MOVE cont.**

COMMENTS cont.

- when the sending item is alphanumeric it is treated, for the purposes of the move, as an unsigned numeric integer.

For an alphabetic receiving field.

- the data is aligned on the leftmost character position with rightmost space fill if the sending item is smaller and rightmost truncation is the sending item is longer.

<u>Group Moves.</u>

A group move is one in which both the sending and receiving fields are group items. Both items are considered to be elementary alphanumeric items and no regard is taken for the individual characteristics of the items subordinate to the group.

EXAMPLES.

```
   .
   01  GRP-FIELD-1.
       03 FIELD-A           PIC 99V99.
       03 FIELD-B           PIC 99V99.
       03 FIELD-C           PIC 99V99.
   .
   01  GRP-FIELD-2.
       03 FIELD-A           PIC 99.99.
       03 FIELD-Z           PIC 99.
       03 FIELD-C           PIC 99.99.
   .
   01  TAB-AREA.
       03 TAB-ENT OCCURS 10 TIMES PIC 99.
   .
   .
       MOVE TAB-ENT (3) TO FIELD-Z.
       MOVE CORRESPONDING GRP-FIELD-1 TO GRP-FIELD-2.
```

PROCEDURE DIVISION   **MOVE cont.**

EXAMPLES cont.

SENDING ITEM		RECEIVING ITEM	
PICTURE	CONTENTS	PICTURE	CONTENTS
99V99	12.34	9V99	2.34
99V99	01.23	S9V9	+1.2
99V99	01.23	Z9.99	1.23
XXXXX	AB123	XXX	AB1
XXX	ABC	XXXXX	ABC
XXXX	AB12	XX/XX	AB/12
AAA	ABC	XXXXX	ABC
AAAAA	ABCDE	XXX	ABC

Further examples relating to exact contents of data-items under certain PICTURE conditions are given on Pages 80 to 82.

NOTES.

PROCEDURE DIVISION   **MULTIPLY**

FORMAT.

1. <u>MULTIPLY</u> {identifier-1 / literal-1} <u>BY</u> identifier-2 [<u>ROUNDED</u>]

                                  [identifier-3 [<u>ROUNDED</u>]]...

               [<u>ON</u> <u>SIZE</u> <u>ERROR</u> imperative-statement]

2. <u>MULTIPLY</u> {identifier-1 / literal-1} <u>BY</u> identifier-2 / literal-2

                  <u>GIVING</u> identifier-3 [<u>ROUNDED</u>]

                        [identifier-4 [<u>ROUNDED</u>]]...

               [<u>ON</u> <u>SIZE</u> <u>ERROR</u> imperative-statement]

COMMENTS.

The MULTIPLY statement causes numeric items to be multiplied and the product placed in result fields.

In Format 1 the product of identifier-1 (or literal-1) and identifier-2 is calculated and the result placed in identifier-2. Multiple calculations may also be performed whereby identifier-1 (or literal-1) is also multiplied by identifier-3 etc., and the result placed in identifier-3 etc.

In Format 2 the product of identifier-1 (or literal-1) and identifier-2 (or literal-2) is calculated and the result placed in identifier-3, identifier-4 etc.

The ROUNDED option rounds the result to the nearest character as described in the receiving fields PICTURE.

The ON SIZE ERROR option allows an imperative statement to be executed should the result overflow the receiving field.

PROCEDURE DIVISION   **MULTIPLY cont.**

EXAMPLES.

```
MULTIPLY FLD-1 BY FLD-2.
MULTIPLY FLD-1 BY 2 GIVING FLD-2.
MULTIPLY 2 BY FLD-1 ON SIZE ERROR GO TO END-PROG.
MULTIPLY 2 BY 3 GIVING FLD-4 FLD-5 FLD-6.
MULTIPLY FLD-1 BY FLD-2 GIVING FLD-3 ROUNDED.
MULTIPLY 2 BY FLD-1 FLD-2.
```

NOTES.

PROCEDURE DIVISION   **OPEN**

FORMAT.

1. OPEN $\left\{\begin{array}{l}\text{INPUT file-name-1}\left[\begin{array}{l}\text{REVERSED}\\\text{WITH NO REWIND}\end{array}\right]\\\quad\quad[\text{file-name-2}\left[\begin{array}{l}\text{REVERSED}\\\text{WITH NO REWIND}\end{array}\right]]\ldots\\\text{OUTPUT file-name-3 [WITH NO REWIND]}\\\quad\quad[\text{file-name-4 [WITH NO REWIND]}]\ldots\\\text{I-O file-name-5 [file-name-6]}\ldots\\\text{EXTEND file-name-7 [file-name-8]}\ldots\end{array}\right\}\ldots$

2. OPEN $\left\{\begin{array}{l}\text{INPUT file-name-1 [file-name-2]}\ldots\\\text{OUTPUT file-name-3 [file-name-4]}\ldots\\\text{I-O file-name-5 [file-name-6]}\ldots\end{array}\right\}\ldots$

COMMENTS.

The OPEN statement initiates the processing of files and performs the checking or writing of labels and other input/output operations.

Each file must be opened before any statement may be executed which refers to that file. This does not apply to SORT or MERGE files which are not opened. Any file opened in a program must be defined in the File Section with an FD file description entry.

Each file should be CLOSED at the end of its processing cycle within a program, although it may be re-opened.

Format 1 refers to sequential files and Format 2 to relative and indexed files.

<u>Sequential Files</u>.

The INPUT phrase specifies that an already created file is to be opened for input operations. If the REVERSED or NO REWIND options are not included the file is positioned at its beginning. The NO REWIND option does not cause the file to be repositioned at the beginning

PROCEDURE DIVISION   **OPEN cont.**

COMMENTS cont.

upon execution of the OPEN statement. In this case the file should already be positioned at the beginning prior to the execution of the OPEN statement. The REVERSED option positions the file at its end and facilitates reverse order reading with each READ statement executed. The REVERSED and NO REWIND options may only be specified for single reel files. If the file does not already exist, or is unavailable, an execution error occurs.

The OUTPUT phrase causes a file to be made available for output operations. If the file does not already exist it will be created. If the file already exists it must not contain any records.

The I-O phrase allows the opening of a file for input or output operations and may only be specified for mass storage files. The file must already exist for this operation to be carried out.

The EXTEND phrase opens a file for output operations and positions the file at its end so that subsequent WRITE operations will append to the file. If the file does not exist it will be created.

<u>Indexed and Relative Files</u>.

Format 2 of the OPEN statement refers to indexed and relative files.

For indexed files OPEN INPUT or I-O opens the file with the record pointer set to the record with the lowest key value. The OUTPUT phrase opens the file for output operations.

A table of allowable statements which may be executed upon files in certain open modes is shown on the following page.

PROCEDURE DIVISION   **OPEN cont.**

COMMENTS cont.

File Access Mode	Statement	Input	Output	Input-Output
SEQUENTIAL	READ	X		X
	WRITE		X	
	REWRITE			X
	START	X		X
	DELETE			X
RANDOM	READ	X		X
	WRITE		X	X
	REWRITE			X
	START			
	DELETE			X
DYNAMIC	READ	X		X
	WRITE		X	X
	REWRITE			X
	START	X		
	DELETE			X

Permissible Statements.

EXAMPLES.

   .
   OPEN OUTPUT PRINT-FILE.
   OPEN INPUT TAPE-FILE-1 REVERSED
        TAPE-FILE-2 WITH NO REWIND.
   OPEN EXTEND APPEND-FILE.
   .
   OPEN INPUT IND-FILE.
   OPEN I-O UPDATE-FILE.

NOTES.

PROCEDURE DIVISION   **PERFORM**

FORMAT.

1. <u>PERFORM</u> procedure-name-1 $\left[\begin{Bmatrix} \text{THROUGH} \\ \text{THRU} \end{Bmatrix} \text{procedure-name-2}\right]$

   $\left[\begin{Bmatrix} \text{identifier} \\ \text{integer} \end{Bmatrix} \underline{\text{TIMES}}\right]$
   $[\underline{\text{UNTIL}} \text{ condition}]$

2. <u>PERFORM</u> procedure-name-1 $\left[\begin{Bmatrix} \text{THROUGH} \\ \text{THRU} \end{Bmatrix} \text{procedure-name-2}\right]$

   <u>VARYING</u> $\begin{Bmatrix} \text{index-name-1} \\ \text{identifier-1} \end{Bmatrix}$ <u>FROM</u> $\begin{Bmatrix} \text{index-name-2} \\ \text{literal-1} \\ \text{identifier-2} \end{Bmatrix}$

   <u>BY</u> $\begin{Bmatrix} \text{literal-2} \\ \text{identifier-3} \end{Bmatrix}$ <u>UNTIL</u> condition-1

   [<u>AFTER</u> $\begin{Bmatrix} \text{index-name-3} \\ \text{identifier-4} \end{Bmatrix}$ <u>FROM</u> $\begin{Bmatrix} \text{index-name-4} \\ \text{literal-3} \\ \text{identifier-5} \end{Bmatrix}$

   <u>BY</u> $\begin{Bmatrix} \text{literal-4} \\ \text{identifier-6} \end{Bmatrix}$ <u>UNTIL</u> condition-2

   [<u>AFTER</u> $\begin{Bmatrix} \text{index-name-5} \\ \text{identifier-7} \end{Bmatrix}$ <u>FROM</u> $\begin{Bmatrix} \text{index-name-6} \\ \text{literal-5} \\ \text{identifier-8} \end{Bmatrix}$

   <u>BY</u> $\begin{Bmatrix} \text{literal-6} \\ \text{identifier-9} \end{Bmatrix}$ <u>UNTIL</u> condition-3]]

COMMENTS.

The PERFORM statement is used to transfer control to one or more procedures, and following the execution of those procedures to return control to the statement following the PERFORM statement.

The procedure-names refer to a section or paragraph in the Procedure Division.

PROCEDURE DIVISION **PERFORM cont.**

COMMENTS cont.

Format 1 will perform a procedure or inclusive range of procedures a certain number of times or until a certain condition becomes true. When the PERFORM statement is executed control is passed to the first statement in procedure-name-1. The execution will then continue through to the last statement in procedure-name-1 (or procedure-name-2, if stated) after which control will pass back to the statement immediately following the PERFORM statement. If the TIMES option is used the process will be repeated the stated number of times, and if the UNTIL option is used the process will be repeated until the condition becomes true.

Although PERFORM's may be nested, if control is passed outside the range of the PERFORM by a GO TO statement then an execution error will appear.

When nesting PERFORM statements the sequence of procedures associated with the included PERFORM must be totally included in, or totally excluded from, the logical sequence referred to by the first PERFORM. Also two such PERFORMs may not share a common end-point.

Format 2 will perform a range of procedures a certain number of times varying a data-item from an initial value, by a specified value until a stated condition becomes true. The AFTER clause allows up to three data items to be varied until the conditions become true and control is returned. This kind of operation is normally used in dealing with two and three dimensional tables.

Both format 1 and format 2 allow zero repetitions, and where terminating conditions are used it is important to note that evaluation takes place before the execution of the range.

PROCEDURE DIVISION   **PERFORM** cont.

EXAMPLES.
```
    PERFORM PARA-1 THRU PARA-3 6 TIMES.

    PERFORM PARA-2 UNTIL REC-COUNTER = 10.

    PERFORM PARA-2 THRU PARA-3 VARYING ITEM-A FROM 1
                              BY 1 UNTIL ITEM-A = 100.

    PERFORM TABLE-CLEAR VARYING SUB2 FROM 1 BY 1 UNTIL
                                               SUB2 = 10
                AFTER SUB1 FROM 1 BY 1 UNTIL SUB1 = 10.


PARA-1.

PARA-2.
    PERFORM PARA-99.
PARA-3.



TABLE-CLEAR.
    MOVE ZERO TO TABLE-ELEMENT (SUB1, SUB2).

```

NOTES.

PROCEDURE DIVISION   **READ**

FORMAT.

1. READ file-name [NEXT] RECORD [INTO identifier]

                    [AT END imperative-statement]

2. READ file-name RECORD [INTO identifier]

         [KEY IS data-name]

         [INVALID KEY imperative-statement]

COMMENTS.

The READ statement makes the next logical record available for sequential files, and for relative and indexed files makes the specified record available.

For a READ statement to be successfully executed the associated file must have been opened for INPUT or I-O. The file-name must have been defined in the File Section.

The INTO option specifies that the record retrieved is to be placed in an identifier specified in the Working-Storage Section, the Linkage Section or in a record-description associated with a previously opened file.

Sequential Files.

Sequential files are read using Format 1 except that the NEXT option is not used.

The READ statement makes available the next logical record from the specified file and updates the value in the FILE STATUS entry, if specified.

If at the time of the execution of the READ statement no next logical record is found then the AT END imperative-statement is invoked and the FILE STATUS item accordingly updated. If no AT END statement is present at this time then an execution error occurs.

Relative Files.

For relative files under sequential access the READ statement makes available the next logical record. For relative files under random access the READ statement

PROCEDURE DIVISION   **READ cont.**

COMMENTS cont.

makes a specified record available.

Relative files may use Format 1 or Format 2 except that the KEY IS option may not be used.

Format 1 is used for files being accessed sequentially. For files in dynamic access mode yet being accessed sequentially the NEXT option must be specified.

Format 2 is used for files in random or dynamic access mode when they are being retrieved randomly.

An INVALID KEY phrase or AT END phrase must be specified for files which do not have a USE procedure specified in the DECLARATIVES.

When Format 2 is used the record made available is that whose relative record number is contained in the data item name in the RELATIVE KEY phrase in the SELECT clause.

Indexed Files.

For indexed files under sequential access the READ statement makes available the next logical record. For indexed files under random access the READ statement makes a specified record available.

Indexed files may use Format 1 or Format 2.

Format 1 is used for files in sequential access mode. For files in dynamic access mode yet being retrieved sequentially the NEXT option must be used.

Format 2 is used for indexed files being retrieved randomly that are in dynamic or random access modes.

When Format 2 is used the record made available is that whose key is equal to the value placed in the KEY IS data-name. If no such record can be found then the INVALID KEY imperative-statement is invoked.

PROCEDURE DIVISION   **READ cont.**

EXAMPLES.

```
READ SEQ-FILE INTO REC-AREA    AT END GO TO CLOSE-DOWN.


                                              Relative file
MOVE REC-NO TO REL-KEY                        with random
READ REL-FILE INVALID KEY GO TO ERROR-R       access.


MOVE "100" TO REC-KEY.                        Indexed file
READ IND-FILE KEY IS REC-KEY                  with random
              INVALID KEY GO TO END-IT.       access.
```

NOTES.

PROCEDURE DIV.   **RECEIVE, SEND, ACCEPT MESSAGE COUNT**

FORMAT.

    RECEIVE cd-name-1 MESSAGE INTO identifier-1

        [NO DATA imperative-statement-1 [END-RECEIVE]]

    SEND cd-name-2 [FROM identifier-2] WITH $\begin{Bmatrix} EMI \\ EGI \end{Bmatrix}$

    $\left[\begin{Bmatrix} BEFORE \\ AFTER \end{Bmatrix} ADVANCING \begin{Bmatrix} \begin{Bmatrix} identifier\text{-}3 \\ integer\text{-}1 \end{Bmatrix} \begin{bmatrix} LINE \\ LINES \end{bmatrix} \\ PAGE \end{Bmatrix} \right]$

    ACCEPT cd-name-3 MESSAGE COUNT

COMMENTS.

The RECEIVE, SEND and ACCEPT MESSAGE COUNT are the Procedure Division verbs used in conjunction with the ANSI level 1 Communication feature of COBOL. All three verbs require CD entries in the Communication Section. (See Pages 46 to 53).

RECEIVE requires a CD input or input-output entry in the Communication Section. Upon execution of the RECEIVE statement the Message Control System (MCS) makes data available to identifier-1. The source of the data is defined for input CD as the SYMBOLIC QUEUE and for input-output CD as the SYMBOLIC TERMINAL. The NO DATA phrase is used to instigate the use of an imperative statement should no message be found available upon execution of a RECEIVE statement.

The SEND verb requires an output CD or input-output CD entry in the Communication Section. It directs a message to be sent out to the specified device. The device is specified for output CD as the SYMBOLIC DESTINATION and for input-output CD as the SYMBOLIC TERMINAL. The TEXT LENGTH must also be specified in both cases. The EMI and EGI options will indicate to the MCS, end-of message and end-of message-group respectively.

PROCEDURE DIV.   RECEIVE, SEND, ACCEPT MESSAGE COUNT

COMMENTS cont.

The ADVANCING clause allow the vertical positioning of
the message on the output device.

The ACCEPT MESSAGE COUNT causes the number of completed
message in a queue to be made available to the MESSAGE
COUNT area associated with the input CD. This
statement can only be used with the input CD entry.

EXAMPLES.

```
    .
    MOVE Q-NAME TO Q-FIELD.
    RECEIVE IN-AREA MESSAGE INTO W-S-AREA-1
        NO DATA PERFORM ERR-PARA.
    .
    .
    SEND OUT-AREA FROM W-S-AREA-2 WITH EMI
        AFTER ADVANCING PAGE.
    .
    .
    ACCEPT IN-AREA MESSAGE COUNT.
    IF MSG-COUNT = 0 GO TO END-POINT.
    .
    .
```

More examples can be found in Communication Section,
Pages 46 to 53.

NOTES.

PROCEDURE DIVISION   **RELEASE**

FORMAT.

    RELEASE record-name [FROM identifier]

COMMENTS.

The RELEASE statement is used in association with the Sort-Merge capabilities of COBOL and transfers records into the initial phase of a SORT operation.

The RELEASE statement may only be specified within an Input Procedure associated with a SORT statement. Within an Input Procedure at least one RELEASE statement must be specified. The record-name must specify a record associated with the SD entry for the sort file.

The FROM option allows the record released to be extracted from the specified identifier.

EXAMPLE.

In the example below SORTWORK is the SD sort file, FILE-IN is the input file and FILE-OUT is the output file. This section of code will sort the input file and extract records with a catalogue number of zeros.

```
    .
    SORT SORTWORK ASCENDING KEY PART-NO
        INPUT PROCEDURE IS EXTRACT
        GIVING FILE-OUT.
    .
 EXTRACT SECTION.
 READ-P.
    READ FILE-IN AT END GO TO READ-P-EX.
    MOVE IN-REC TO SORT-REC.
    IF CAT-NO NOT EQUAL TO ZEROS
        RELEASE SORT-REC
        GO TO READ-P.
 READ-P-EX.
    EXIT.
```

NOTES.

PROCEDURE DIVISION   **RETURN**

FORMAT.

    <u>RETURN</u> file-name RECORD [<u>INTO</u> identifier]

                          [AT <u>END</u> imperative-statement]

COMMENTS.

The RETURN statement obtains either sorted records from the final phase of a SORT operation or merged records during a MERGE operation.

The file-name specified must be one described by a SD sort-merge file description in the File Section.

The RETURN statement may only be used within the range of an output procedure associated with a SORT or MERGE statement. This statement makes records available prior to release to the output file.

When the INTO option is used the data is made available to the stored identifier as well as to the input record area. The AT END statement indicates an imperative-statement execution upon the AT END condition of the sort-merge workfile.

EXAMPLE.

In the example below SORTWORK is the sort file, FILE-IN is the input file and FILE-OUT is the output file. This section of code will sort the input file and produce the output file although all records with a catalogue number of greater than 1000 will be displayed on the console.
-
-

      SORT SORTWORK ON ASCENDING KEY PART-NO
      USING FILE-IN
      OUTPUT PROCEDURE IS DISPLAY-IT.
-
-
-
-

PROCEDURE DIVISION   **RETURN cont.**

EXAMPLES cont.
   .
   DISPLAY-IT SECTION.
   WRITE-IT.
       RETURN SORTWORK AT END GO TO WRITE-IT-EX.
       WRITE REC-OUT FROM REC-WORK.
       IF CAT-NO 1000 > DISPLAY REC-WORK.
       GO TO WRITE-IT.
   WRITE-IT-EX.
       EXIT.
       .
       .

NOTES.

PROCEDURE DIVISION   **REWRITE**

FORMAT.

REWRITE record-name [FROM identifier]

                 [INVALID KEY imperative-statement]

COMMENTS.

The REWRITE statement is used to logically replace a disk-file record in-situ. The file must have been opened for I-O.

The FROM option has the effect of moving the record from the identifier to the record-name prior to the rewrite.

The FILE STATUS clause, when specified, is updated by the REWRITE statement.

Sequential Files.

In the case of sequential files the last successful input-output operation on the associated file must have been a READ statement. The REWRITE statement will logically replace the record obtained by the READ statement.

The INVALID KEY option may not be used with sequentially organised files.

Relative Files.

The record replaced when the access mode is random or dynamic for relative files is that one specified by the RELATIVE KEY data item. If that record is not found the INVALID KEY imperative-statement is executed.

For sequential access the INVALID KEY option must not be specified. In this case the record replaced is that one obtained by the last successful READ operation.

Indexed Files.

For random and dynamic access of an indexed file the record replaced is that one specified by the RECORD KEY data item. If no such record can be found the INVALID KEY imperative-statement is executed.

PROCEDURE DIVISION   **REWRITE cont.**

COMMENTS cont.

For sequential access the INVALID KEY option must also be used. The last successful input-output operation must have been a READ and the record replaced is the one with a key corresponding to the current RECORD KEY data item. If this record is not found the INVALID KEY clause is invoked.

EXAMPLE.

```
    .
    OPEN I-O SEQ-FILE.
    .
    READ SEQ-FILE INTO W-S-AREA AT END GO TO EOF.
    IF ITEM-1 = ZERO
        ADD 10 TO ITEM-2
        REWRITE SEQ-REC FROM W-S-AREA.
    .
    OPEN I-O REL-FILE
         INPUT AMEND-FILE.
    .
    READ AMEND-FILE AT END GO TO EOF.
    MOVE AMEND-REC-NO TO RELATIVE-KEY.
    MOVE REST-REC TO REST-REL-REC.
    REWRITE REL-REC
            INVALID KEY DISPLAY "AMEND REC NOT FOUND"
                                            GO TO EOF.
```

NOTES.

PROCEDURE DIVISION   **SEARCH**

FORMAT.

1. <u>SEARCH</u> identifier-1 [<u>VARYING</u> $\begin{Bmatrix} \text{index-name-1} \\ \text{identifier-2} \end{Bmatrix}$

    [AT <u>END</u> imperative-statement]

      <u>WHEN</u> condition-1 $\begin{Bmatrix} \text{imperative-statement-2} \\ \underline{\text{NEXT}}\ \underline{\text{SENTENCE}} \end{Bmatrix}$

      [<u>WHEN</u> condition-2 $\begin{Bmatrix} \text{imperative-statement-3} \\ \underline{\text{NEXT}}\ \underline{\text{SENTENCE}} \end{Bmatrix}$]...

2. <u>SEARCH</u> ALL identifier-1

    [AT <u>END</u> imperative-statement-1]

    <u>WHEN</u> $\begin{Bmatrix} \text{data-name-1} \begin{Bmatrix} \text{IS} = \\ \text{IS } \underline{\text{EQUAL}} \text{ TO} \end{Bmatrix} \begin{Bmatrix} \text{identifier-3} \\ \text{literal-1} \\ \text{arithmetic-exp-1} \end{Bmatrix} \\ \text{condition-name-1} \end{Bmatrix}$

    [<u>AND</u> $\begin{Bmatrix} \text{data-name-2} \begin{Bmatrix} \text{IS} = \\ \text{IS } \underline{\text{EQUAL}} \text{ TO} \end{Bmatrix} \begin{Bmatrix} \text{identifier-4} \\ \text{literal-1} \\ \text{arithmetic-exp-2} \end{Bmatrix} \\ \text{condition-name-2} \end{Bmatrix}$]...

    $\begin{Bmatrix} \text{imperative-statement-2} \\ \underline{\text{NEXT}}\ \underline{\text{STATEMENT}} \end{Bmatrix}$

COMMENTS.

The SEARCH statement is used to search a table for a certain table element that satisfies a specified condition and to adjust an associated index-name to indicate that table element.

Identifier-1 refers to the table-name. That is, it's description must contain an OCCURS clause with the INDEXED BY option, but it may not be subscripted or indexed. The identifier-1 associated with format 2 must also have the KEY IS phrase associated with it's OCCURS clause.

Format 1 refers to a serial search and Format 2 to a non-serial search. The usage of the SEARCH statement may vary, and implementation manuals should be consulted.

PROCEDURE DIVISION   **SEARCH cont.**

COMMENTS cont.

Serial Search.

The serial search is specified by Format 1. The table, indicated by identifier-1 is searched, incrementing it's associated index-name-1 or identifier-2, until the specified condition(s) become true.

The AT END imperative-statement is invoked when the indexing variable is incremented beyond the number of table elements as specified by the OCCURS clause.

Index-name-1 or identifier-2 is initialised using the SET verb.

When the specified condition(s) become true and the required table element is found control passes to the NEXT SENTENCE or the associated imperative-statement.

Non-Serial Search.

The non-serial search is specified by Format 2. No associated index-name or identifier needs to be set as the setting of the search-index is varied throughout the non-serial search.

If the conditions cannot be satisfied and the table element cannot be found the AT END imperative-statement is invoked.

When the associated condition(s) become true control is passed to NEXT SENTENCE or imperative-statement-2.

EXAMPLE.

1. Serial Search.
```
        .
        01   TAB-AREA-2.
             03 TABLE-1 OCCURS 50 TIMES INDEXED BY TAB-VAR.
        .
        .
        .
             SET TAB-VAR TO 1.
             SEARCH TABLE-1 VARYING TAB-VAR
                         AT END GO TO NOT-FOUND
                         WHEN TAB-ENTRY (TAB-VAR) = 99
                         GO TO FOUND.
```

PROCEDURE DIVISION   **SEARCH cont.**

EXAMPLES cont.

2. Non-Serial Search.
    .
    01   TAB-AREA-2.
         03 TABLE-2 OCCURS 50 TIMES ASCENDING KEY IS
                                    TAB-VAR2
                                    INDEXED BY TAB-VAR2.
    .
    .
         SEARCH ALL TABLE-2
                 AT END GO TO NOT-FOUND
                 WHEN TAB-ENTRY2 (TAB-VAR2) = 99
                 GO TO FOUND.

NOTES.

PROCEDURE DIVISION   **SET**

FORMAT.

1. <u>SET</u> {identifier-1   [identifier-2]...}
       {index-name-1 [index-name-2]...}

                        <u>TO</u> {identifier-3}
                            {index-name-3}
                            {integer-1   }

2. <u>SET</u>   index-name-1   [index-name-2]...

                 {<u>UP</u>   <u>BY</u>} {indentifier-4}
                 {<u>DOWN</u> <u>BY</u>} {integer-2   }

COMMENTS.

The SET statement initialises index-names associated with table-elements. These index-names are used in table handling operations using SEARCH and PERFORM statements.

The index-names are related to the table by the INDEXED BY option of the OCCURS clause.

In Format 1, identifier-1 or index-name-1 etc., are set to the values given by identifier-3, index-name-3 or integer-1.

In Format 2, index-name-1, index-name-2 etc. are incremented (UP BY) or decremented (DOWN BY) the value specified by identifier-4 or integer-2.

EXAMPLES.

- SET INDEX-1 TO 1.
- SET INDEX-2 UP BY FIELD-2.
-

NOTES.

PROCEDURE DIVISION   **SORT**

FORMAT.

SORT file-name-1 ON $\begin{Bmatrix} \underline{\text{ASCENDING}} \\ \underline{\text{DESCENDING}} \end{Bmatrix}$ KEY data-name-1 [data-name-2]...

[ON $\begin{Bmatrix} \underline{\text{ASCENDING}} \\ \underline{\text{DESCENDING}} \end{Bmatrix}$ KEY data-name-3 [data-name-4]...]...

[COLLATING <u>SEQUENCE</u> IS alphabet-name]

$\begin{Bmatrix} \underline{\text{INPUT PROCEDURE}} \text{ IS section-name-1} \\ \qquad\qquad [\begin{matrix}\underline{\text{THROUGH}}\\ \underline{\text{THRU}}\end{matrix}\ \text{section-name-2}] \\ \underline{\text{USING}}\ \text{file-name-2 [file-name-3]...} \end{Bmatrix}$

$\begin{Bmatrix} \underline{\text{OUTPUT PROCEDURE}} \text{ IS section-name-3} \\ \qquad\qquad [\begin{matrix}\underline{\text{THROUGH}}\\ \underline{\text{THRU}}\end{matrix}\ \text{section-name-4}] \\ \underline{\text{GIVING}}\ \text{file-name-4} \end{Bmatrix}$

COMMENTS.

The SORT statement accepts records from one or more specified files, sorts them according to a set of keys and makes the records available through an output procedure or an output file. The major keys are listed first.

File-name-1 refers to a file which must be described with an SD (sort-merge file description) in the File Section of the program.

If the USING option is used then file-name-2, file-name-3 represent the files to be sorted and must be described with FD (file description) entries in the File Section. The size of the records associated with these files must be equal to the size of the logical record associated with the sort workfile (file-name-1).

No files associated with the SORT should be open prior to it's execution. The SORT function automatically opens and closes all associated files.

PROCEDURE DIVISION   **SORT cont.**

COMMENTS cont.

The INPUT PROCEDURE may refer to a Section or series of consecutive sections in which procedures may reside which select, create or modify records prior to the sequencing of file-name-1 by the SORT statement. The input procedure must contain at least one RELEASE statement to release the records to the SORT. (See Page 147).

The GIVING option indicates the name of the file into which the sorted records are placed. The specified file must be described by an FD entry and should not be open prior to the execution of the SORT.

The OUTPUT PROCEDURE specifies a Section or series of consecutive sections in which procedures may reside which select, modify or copy records as they are returned from the SORT. The output procedures must contain at lease one RETURN statement to make the records available for processing. (See Page 148).

The COLLATING SEQUENCE option specifies the collating sequence to be used in the nonnumeric comparisons of the key values. The alphabet-name must be specified in the SPECIAL-NAMES paragraph.

EXAMPLES.

```
    .
    FILE SECTION.
    SD   SORT-FILE
         DATA RECORD IS SORT-REC.
    01   SORT REC.
         03 INV-NO        PIC X(6).
           .
           .
           .
    FD   IN-FILE
           .
    FD   OUT-FILE
           .
    PROCEDURE DIVISION.
    PARA-1.
         SORT SORT-FILE ON ASCENDING INV-NO
             USING IN-FILE
             GIVING OUT-FILE.
           .
```

PROCEDURE DIVISION   **START**

FORMAT.

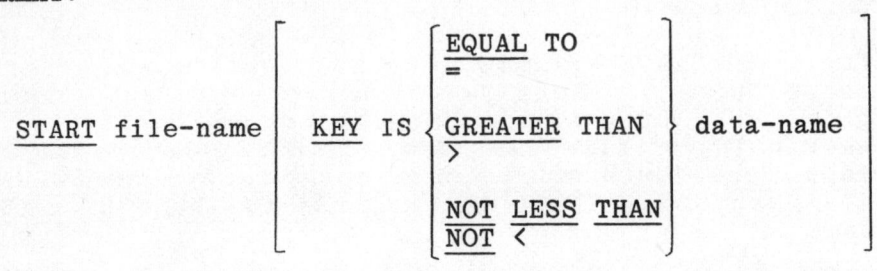

$$\underline{\text{START}}\ \text{file-name}\ \left[\ \underline{\text{KEY}}\ \text{IS}\ \left\{\begin{array}{l}\underline{\text{EQUAL TO}}\\=\\\underline{\text{GREATER THAN}}\\>\\\underline{\text{NOT LESS THAN}}\\\underline{\text{NOT}}\ <\end{array}\right\}\ \text{data-name}\ \right]$$

[<u>INVALID</u> KEY imperative-statement]

COMMENTS.

The START verb is used to arrange for sequential processing of an indexed file to begin at a particular key, rather than at the beginning of the file. Processing will then continue sequentially until another START verb is encountered, or a CLOSE statement is encountered, or the end of file is reached.

If the indexed file is to be read sequentially from the beginning then a START verb is not required before the READ statement.

EXAMPLE.

```
    .
    .
    SELECT FILE-A ASSIGN TO DISK
    ORGANISATION IS INDEXED
    ACCESS MODE IS SEQUENTIAL
    RECORD KEY IS ENTRY-NO.
    .
    .
    .
    PROCEDURE DIVISION.
        OPEN INPUT FILE-A.
        MOVE "900" TO ENTRY-NO.
        START FILE-A KEY = ENTRY-NO INVALID KEY PERFORM
                                                 ERROR-END.
    .
    READ-PARA.
        READ FILE-A AT END GO TO READ-END.
    .
        GO TO READ-PARA.
    .
```

NOTES.

PROCEDURE DIVISION   **STOP**

FORMAT.

$$\underline{\text{STOP}} \left\{ \begin{array}{l} \text{literal} \\ \underline{\text{RUN}} \end{array} \right\}$$

COMMENTS.

The STOP verb is used to terminate the execution of an object program.

When the RUN option is used the execution of the object program is terminated and control is returned to the system.

When the literal option is used the literal is displayed on the operator's console. The operator can then resume the program from the point at which it stopped, if required.

EXAMPLES.
-
-
-
-
```
    IF INTERUP-CODE = 99
            STOP "PROGRAM HALT 99 - RESUME PROGRAM"
    ELSE
            STOP RUN.
```

NOTES.

PROCEDURE DIVISION   **STRING**

FORMAT.

$$\underline{\text{STRING}} \left\{ \begin{matrix} \text{identifier-1} \\ \text{literal-1} \end{matrix} \right\} \left[\begin{matrix} \text{identifier-2} \\ \text{literal-2} \end{matrix} \right] \ldots$$

$$\underline{\text{DELIMITED BY}} \left\{ \begin{matrix} \text{identifier-3} \\ \text{literal-3} \\ \underline{\text{SIZE}} \end{matrix} \right\}$$

$$\left[\left\{ \begin{matrix} \text{identifier-4} \\ \text{literal-4} \end{matrix} \right\} \left[\begin{matrix} \text{identifier-5} \\ \text{literal-5} \end{matrix} \right] \ldots \right.$$

$$\left. \underline{\text{DELIMITED BY}} \left\{ \begin{matrix} \text{identifier-6} \\ \text{literal-6} \\ \underline{\text{SIZE}} \end{matrix} \right\} \right] \ldots$$

$$\underline{\text{INTO}} \text{ identifier-7 [WITH } \underline{\text{POINTER}} \text{ identifier-8]}$$

[ON <u>OVERFLOW</u> imperative-statement]

COMMENTS.

The STRING statement provides the ability to put together the partial or complete contents of two or more data items into a single data item.

All literals must be nonnumeric and figurative constants may be used. When a figurative constant is used it is considered to be 1 character nonnumeric.

Identifier-7 must be an elementary alphanumeric data item. All identifiers must have a DISPLAY usage.

Identifier-1, identifier-2, identifier-4, identifier-5 or their corresponding literals are the sending fields and identifier-7 is the receiving field.

The DELIMITED BY phrase specifies the characters delimiting the data to be transferred. The key word SIZE specifies that the complete sending area is to be transferred.

The POINTER field is an elementary numeric data item which may be used to define the number of characters to be transferred. The field must be set, prior to execution of the string, to the number of characters to be moved plus 1.

The ON OVERFLOW imperative statement is invoked should the pointer field, which may be explicitly or

PROCEDURE DIVISION   **STRING cont.**

COMMENTS cont.

implicitly defined and is incremented by each character's move, have a value exceeding the number of characters in the receiving field or less than 1.

EXAMPLE.

```
    01 EMP-REC.
       03 EMP-NAM            PIC X(10).
       03 EMP-ADD            PIC X(20).
       03 EMP-NO             PIC 9(5).
       03 SALARY-GRADE       PIC XXX.

    01 AREA-A                PIC X(50) VALUE SPACES.

       STRING "EMP. NAME " EMP-NAM
              "EMP. NUMBER " EMP-NO
              " SALARY GRADE " SALARY GRADE
              DELIMITED BY SIZE
              INTO AREA-A.
       DISPLAY AREA-A.
```

would give

EMP. NAME JOE SMITH EMP. NUMBER 12345 SALARY GRADE 74D

NOTES.

PROCEDURE DIVISION   **SUBTRACT**

FORMAT.

1. SUBTRACT $\begin{Bmatrix} \text{identifier-1} \\ \text{literal-1} \end{Bmatrix} \begin{bmatrix} \text{identifier-2} \\ \text{literal-2} \end{bmatrix} \ldots$

      FROM identifier-m [ROUNDED]
                       [identifier-n [ROUNDED]]...

      [ON SIZE ERROR imperative-statement]

2. SUBTRACT $\begin{Bmatrix} \text{identifier-1} \\ \text{literal-1} \end{Bmatrix} \begin{bmatrix} \text{identifier-2} \\ \text{literal-2} \end{bmatrix} \ldots$

      FROM $\begin{Bmatrix} \text{identifier-m} \\ \text{literal-m} \end{Bmatrix}$

      GIVING identifier-n [ROUNDED]
                      [identifier-o[ROUNDED]]...

      [ON SIZE ERROR imperative-statement]

3. SUBTRACT $\begin{Bmatrix} \text{CORRESPONDING} \\ \text{CORR} \end{Bmatrix}$ identifier-1

      FROM identifier-2 [ROUNDED]

      [ON SIZE ERROR imperative-statement]

COMMENTS.

The SUBTRACT statement is used to subtract one, or the sum of two or more, numeric data items from one or more data items, and set the values of one or more items to the results.

Format 1 will subtract one, or the sum of two or more data-items from a data-item and place the results into the items that have been subtracted from.

Format 2 will subtract one, or the sum of two or more data-items from a data-item and place the results in the items specified by the GIVING phrase.

Format 3 will subtract one group of similarly named items from another group of similarly named items under the rules specified by the CORRESPONDING option on Page 112.

PROCEDURE DIVISION   **SUBTRACT cont.**

COMMENTS cont.

In each case identifier must refer to an elementary numeric data-item except in Format 2 where the GIVING may also specify an elementary numeric edited item and in Format 3 where the indentifiers refer to group items.

Each literal must be a numeric literal.

The ROUNDED option rounds the result to the nearest character as described in the receiving fields PICTURE.

The ON SIZE ERROR option indicates the execution of an imperative-statement should the result overflow the receiving field.

EXAMPLES.

- SUBTRACT A FROM B ROUNDED.
- SUBTRACT A, B, C FROM D GIVING E
              ON SIZE ERROR DISPLAY "ERROR A".
- SUBTRACT CORR F-GROUP FROM G-GROUP.
-

NOTES.

PROCEDURE DIVISION   UNSTRING

FORMAT.

UNSTRING identifier-1

       [<u>DELIMITED</u> BY [<u>ALL</u>] identifier-2
                             literal-1

              [<u>OR</u> [<u>ALL</u>] {identifier-3 / literal-2}]...]

      <u>INTO</u> identifier-4 [<u>DELIMITER</u> IN identifier-5]

                     [<u>COUNT</u> IN identifier-6]

         identifier-7 [<u>DELIMITER</u> IN identifier-8]

                     [<u>COUNT</u> IN identifier-9]]...

      [WITH <u>POINTER</u> identifier-10]

      [<u>TALLYING</u> IN identifier-11]

      [ON <u>OVERFLOW</u> imperative-statement]

COMMENTS.

The UNSTRING statement allows contiguous data in a sending field to be separated and placed in several receiving fields.

All literals must be nonnumeric and figurative constants may be used. When a figurative constant is used it is considered to be 1 character nonnumeric.

Identifier-1 is the sending field and must be an alphanumeric data item.

The DELIMITED BY option specifies delimiters within the data that control the data transfer. Each specified delimiter must be an alphanumeric data item. More than one possible delimiter may be specified by the OR option. The ALL option indicates that several consecutive occurrences of the delimiter will be treated as just one occurrence for delimiting purposes.

Identifier-4, identifier-7 etc. are the receiving fields and must have a DISPLAY usage and may be alphabetic, alphanumeric or numeric.

PROCEDURE DIVISION   **UNSTRING cont.**

COMMENTS cont.

The DELIMITER IN option specifies the delimiter receiving field and must be alphanumeric.

The COUNT IN option specifies a numeric data item which will hold the number of characters transferred to each receiving field, excluding the delimiters.

The POINTER option specifies the number of characters to be transferred. The associated data item must be initialized prior to the execution of UNSTRING.

The TALLYING option is used to count the number of receiving fields affected and must be initialized prior to execution.

The ON OVERFLOW imperative-statement is invoked should all the receiving fields be used and yet data is still to be transferred from the sending field.

EXAMPLE.

The field NAME-LINE contains up to 5 surnames, each separated by an "*". Each name is not more than 10 characters long.

```
    01  NAME LINE           PIC X(54).
    01  NO-OF-NAMES         PIC 9 VALUE ZERO.

    01  NAME-PRINT-REC.
        03 N-1              PIC X(10).
        03 N-2              PIC X(10).
        03 N-3              PIC X(10).
        03 N-4              PIC X(10).
        03 N-5              PIC X(10).

        UNSTRING NAME-LINE DELIMITED BY "*"
            INTO N-1 N-2 N-3 N-4 N-5
            TALLYING NO-OF-NAMES
            ON OVERFLOW GO TO ERROR-N.
```

NOTES.

PROCEDURE DIVISION   WRITE

FORMAT.

1. <u>WRITE</u> record-name [<u>FROM</u> identifier]

    [<u>INVALID</u> KEY imperative-statement]

2. <u>WRITE</u> record-name [<u>FROM</u> identifier-1]

    [{<u>BEFORE</u>} ADVANCING { {identifier-2} [LINE] }]
      {<u>AFTER</u> }   { {integer   } [LINES] }
                                  { {mnemonic-name}   }
                                  { {PAGE   }   }

    [AT {<u>END-OF-PAGE</u>} imperative-statement]
        {<u>EOP</u>   }

COMMENTS.

The WRITE statement releases a logical record to an output file or input-output file.

<u>Sequential Files</u>.

For WRITE statements on sequential files Format 2 is used. This form of WRITE also allows positioning of a line vertically within a logical page.

The file must be open for OUTPUT or EXTEND mode at the time of execution of the statement.
The record, once it is written, becomes unavailable in the record area.

The FROM option allows the record to be extracted from the stated identifier prior to the execution of the WRITE statement.

The BEFORE and AFTER options specify the writing of the record before or after a certain action. These actions are a certain number of lines, as specified by identifier-2 or integer, or before or after the advancing of a full PAGE or mnemonic-name feature as defined in the SPECIAL-NAMES paragraph.

The AT END-OF-PAGE option indicates the execution of an imperative-statement at the end of page. The LINAGE clause must be specified in the file description before the END-OF-PAGE facility may be used.

PROCEDURE DIVISION   **WRITE cont.**

COMMENTS cont.

Relative and Indexed Files.

For relative and indexed files Format 1 should be used and the files should be open for OUTPUT or I-O.

For relative files with sequential access the records are released in order with a relative key number starting at 1 for the first record and ascending in steps of 1.

For relative files with dynamic or random access the RELATIVE KEY must contain the desired relative record value.

For indexed files under sequential access the records must be released in ascending order RECORD KEY values.

For indexed files under dynamic or random access the records may be released in any order as specified with the RECORD KEY data-item.

The INVALID KEY option will be invoked should the RECORD or RELATIVE KEY values not adhere to the value required. That is, the key must not specify an area outside the file boundaries or a record which already exists.

EXAMPLES.

. WRITE REL-REC FROM W-S-REC INVALID KEY DISPLAY
                                           "INV KEY".

. WRITE PRINT-REC FROM HEADING-LINE AFTER PAGE.
. WRITE PRINT-REC FROM SUB-HDG AFTER ADVANCING 4 LINES.

NOTES.

GLOSSARY

Alphabet name   A programmer-defined word in the SPECIAL-NAMES paragraph that assigns a name to a specific collating sequence or character set.

Arithmetic Expression   An expression containing a combination of identifiers and numeric literals joined by one or more arithmetic operators in such a way that the whole expression may be reduced to a single numeric value.

Arithmetic operator   A single or fixed double character belonging to the following set

Characters	Meaning
+	addition
-	subtraction
*	multiplication
/	division
**	exponentiation

Block   A physical unit of data that is normally composed of one or more records. The term is synonymous with physical record.

cd-name   A programmer-defined word that defines an MCS interface area as defined in the Communication Section.

Class-Condition   A condition for which a truth value may be determined for an item whose content is wholly alphabetic or wholly numeric.

Collating Sequence   The sequence in which characters are ordered for the purposes of sorting, merging and comparing.

Clock Units   A measure of the number of processing units needed to perform a task within a computer.

Checkpoint Records   A record taken at certain intervals in a machine run which notes the condition of certain variables which may be useful should restart procedures become necessary.

Control Break   Generally a change in the value of a data-item that is used to control the hierarchical structure of a report.

GLOSSARY cont.

<u>Delimiter</u> A character or string of characters that defines the beginning and end of a character string. A delimiter is not part of the string itself.

<u>Dynamic Access</u> An access mode in which logical records may be obtained from or placed into a mass storage file in a non-sequential manner and may be obtained from a file in a sequential manner.

<u>Identifier</u> A data-name, followed by any necessary qualifiers, subscripts or indices, which makes unique reference to a data item.

<u>Imperative Statement</u> A statement, or statements, which direct unconditional action to be taken.

<u>Implementor name</u> A system-name that refers to a particular feature available on that implementor's computing system.

<u>Index</u> A storage position, or register, the contents of which represent the identification of a particular table element.

<u>Index name</u> A programmer-defined word that names an index associated with a particular table.

<u>Index organisation</u> A file structure in which each record is identified by the value of one or more keys within that record.

<u>Integer</u> A numeric literal or numeric data item that does not have any character positions to the right of the assumed decimal point. When specified in format it must be an unsigned, non zero, numeric data item unless otherwise stated.

<u>Invalid key condition</u> A condition caused when a key associated with an indexed or relative file is determined, at run time, to be invalid.

<u>Literal</u> A character-string whose value is implied by the ordered set of characters comprising the string.

<u>Logical operator</u> One of the reserved words AND, OR or NOT. In the formation of a condition AND or OR may be used as logical connectives and NOT may be used for logical negation.

GLOSSARY cont.

Message Control System (MCS) A communication control system that deals with the processing of messages.

Mnemonic-name A programmer-defined word that is associated in the Environment Division with a specified implementor-name.

Object program In the context of this book it is the executable machine language result of the action of the COBOL compiler on a source program.

Object time The time at which the object program is executed.

Operand Generally it is the component of a statement which is operated on. In the specific formats it relates to the lower case words.

Paragraph In the Procedure Division, a paragraph name followed by a period, space and one or more sentences. In the Identification Divisions a paragraph header followed by a zero, one or more entries.

Paragraph header A reserved word followed by a period and a space that indicates the beginning of an entry in the Identification and Environment Divisions (eg. PROGRAM-ID).

Paragraph name A programmer-defined word that indicates the beginning of a paragraph in the Procedure Division.

Procedure name A user-defined word which is used to name a paragraph or section in the Procedure Division.

Pseudo-text A sequence of character-strings and/or separators bounded by pseudo-text delimiters.

Pseudo-text delimiters Special characters used to delimit pseudo-text. (Normally << and >> or == and ==)

Qualifier

1. A data-name used in reference together with one from a lower level in the same hierarchy.

2. A section-name used in reference together with a paragraph-name specified in that section.

GLOSSARY cont.

---

3. A library-name used in reference together with a text-name associated with that library.

<u>Queue</u>   A logical collection of messages awaiting transmission or processing.

<u>Random Access</u>   An access mode in which the value of a key data item identifies the logical record that is obtained from, deleted from or placed into a relative or indexed file.

<u>Relation condition</u>   A condition for which a truth value can be determined should an arithmetic expression or data item have a certain relationship to another arithmetic expression or data item.

<u>Relative organisation</u>   A permanent logical file structure in which each record is uniquely identified by an integer value greater than zero, which identifies the record's logical position in the file.

<u>Section</u>   A combination of words followed by a period and a space that indicate the beginning of a section in the Environment, Data or Procedure Divisions.

<u>Segment number</u>   A programmer-defined word which classifies sections in the Procedure Division for the purposes of segmentation.

<u>Sequential organisation</u>   A permanent logical file structure in which a record is identified by the sequential order in which that record was placed in the file.

<u>Sign condition</u>   A condition for which a truth value may be established when the algebraic value of a data-item or arithmetic expression is either less than, greater than or equal to zero.

<u>Source program</u>   A program which is coded in a non-machine language that must first be translated into machine code before execution.

<u>Statement</u>   A syntactically correct combination of words and symbols written in the Procedure Division and beginning with a verb.

<u>Subscript</u>   An integer whose value identifies a particular table element.

GLOSSARY cont.

<u>Word</u> A character-string of not more than 30 characters which forms a programmer-defined word, a system-name or a reserved word.